New Life/New Walk

New Life/New Walk

by
John MacArthur, Jr.

"GRACE TO YOU"
P.O. Box 4000
Panorama City, CA   91412

All Scripture quotations, unless noted otherwise, are from the *New Scofield
Reference Bible*, King James Version. Copyright © 1967 by Oxford Univer-
sity Press, Inc. Reprinted by permission.

ISBN: 0-8024-5337-6

1 2 3 4 5 6 Printing/LC/Year 94 93 92 91 90

Printed in the United States of America

Contents

These Bible studies are taken from messages delivered by Pastor-Teacher John MacArthur, Jr., at Grace Community Church in Panorama City, California. These messages have been combined into a 6-tape album titled *New Life/New Walk*. You may purchase this series either in an attractive vinyl cassette album or as individual cassettes. To purchase these tapes, request the album *New Life/New Walk*, or ask for the tapes by their individual GC numbers. Please consult the current price list; then, send your order, making your check payable to:

The Master's Communication
P.O. Box 4000
Panorama City, CA 91412

Or call the following toll-free number:
1-800-55-GRACE

1
Off with the Old, On with the New— Part 1

Outline

Introduction
A. The Change of Nature
B. The Character of Newness
C. The Cause of Sin
D. The Concept of Transformation
E. The Context of Paul's Instruction
  1. The principles
     a) Taken generally
     b) Taken specifically
  2. The people
  3. The problem
  4. The parallels

Lesson
I. The Old Walk (vv. 17b-19)
   A. Self-Centeredness (v. 17b)
   B. Ignorance (v. 18)
      1. Darkened understanding
      2. Alienation from God
         a) God's confirmation
         b) Man's rejection
         c) Satan's deception
   C. Shamelessness (v. 19a)
   D. Perversion (v. 19b)

Conclusion

Introduction

A. The Change of Nature

When you receive Jesus Christ and enter into God's kingdom, you become a totally different individual. The change that occurs when you are saved is more dramatic than the change that will occur when you die. Why? Because by the time you die you already have a new nature and you already are a citizen of God's kingdom. All death does is enable you to enter into God's presence.

1. 2 Corinthians 5:17—"If any man be in Christ, he is a new creation; old things are passed away; behold, all things are become new." We don't receive something new—we ourselves become new!

2. Galatians 2:20—Paul said, "I am crucified with Christ: nevertheless I live; yet not I, but Christ liveth in me; and the life which I now live in the flesh I live by the faith of the Son of God, who loved me and gave himself for me."

B. The Character of Newness

In his epistles Paul writes that every believer has been given a new will, mind, heart, life, inheritance, relationship, and citizenship. We also receive new power, knowledge, wisdom, perception, understanding, righteousness, love, and desire. He called it the "newness of life" (Rom. 6:4). Some teach that when a person becomes a Christian, God gives him a new nature in addition to his old sin nature. But according to the Word of God *we* are new. Our new life isn't a matter of an addition; it's a transformation!

C. The Cause of Sin

However, that raises this question: "If I'm such a new creation, why do I still sin?" Christians continue to sin because their new nature is encased in a smelly old coat known as the flesh. In Romans 7:17-18 Paul says, "It is no more I that do it, but sin that dwelleth in me (that is, in my flesh)" (cf. v. 20). When I sin it is not my new nature that sins but the "sin that dwelleth in me." Sin dwells in my humanness—the smelly coat that my new nature has to endure until I go to be with the Lord. In 1 Peter 2:1 the Greek word translated "laying aside" literally means "to strip off clothes." We are to take off the dirty clothes of our flesh and throw them away.

D. The Concept of Transformation

When we become Christians God does not remodel us or add to who we are—we are transformed. I don't believe a Christian has two different natures. He has one new nature —the new nature in Christ. The old self dies and the new self lives; they do not coexist. The new nature is righteous, holy, and sanctified because Christ lives in us (Col. 1:27). He is righteous, holy, and sanctified, and we have the divine principle in us—what Peter called the "incorruptible" seed (1 Pet. 1:23).

Ephesians 4:24 tells us to "put on the new man," a new behavior that is appropriate to our new nature. But to do so we have to eliminate the patterns and practices of our old life. In Colossians 3 the apostle Paul says, "If ye, then, be risen with Christ. . . . [kill], therefore, your members which are upon the earth: fornication, uncleanness, inordinate affection, evil desire, and covetousness" (vv. 1, 5).

E. The Context of Paul's Instruction

The first three chapters of Ephesians discuss the new nature of the new man. From Ephesians 4:17 to the end of the epistle Paul instructs us to change our old life-style to accommodate a new one. Romans 6:13 says, "Neither yield ye your members as instruments of unrighteousness unto sin, but yield yourselves unto God, as those that are alive from the dead, and your members as instruments of righteousness unto God." If we say we are risen with Christ and have been transformed, we should act like it. We are to behave in accord with who we are.

Let's look at how the new nature functions in the new man as we examine Ephesians 4:17-24. Before we do that, however, we need to establish the context of chapter 4.

1. The principles

In verse 1 Paul says, "I therefore, the prisoner of the Lord, beseech you that ye walk worthy of the vocation to which ye are called." How do we walk worthy? Verse 17 says, "This I say, therefore, and testify in the Lord, that ye henceforth walk not as other Gentiles walk." The worthy walk is different from that of the world.

a) Taken generally

"Therefore" in verse 17 refers to Paul's discussion in verses 1-16 about the unity, spiritual maturity, and growth of the church. He talked there in generalities about how the church is to function, but in verse 17 he gets specific about what God wants individual believers to do. We are to walk worthy because of the vocation to which we have been called (v. 1); because God wants us to be humble, meek, and patient (v. 2); because we are one in Christ (vv. 3-6); because He has uniquely gifted us as members of His Body (vv. 7-11); and because He has given the church principles for maturity, growth, edification, and love (vv. 12-16). It's as if Paul had been saying, "God has created a marvelous new entity called the church, with its unique character of humility, its unique empowerment with spiritual gifts, its unique unity as the Body of Christ, and its need to be built up in love. This is how every believer should live as a member of that church."

b) Taken specifically

After discussing what the church is designed to be, Paul presented the specifics of how individual believers are to behave. The first principle is that we are not to live like people in the world. Since we are members of the church of Jesus Christ, we are unique. The world is proud; we are humble. The world is fragmented; we are united. The world is impotent; we are gifted. The world is hateful; we are full of love. The world doesn't know the truth; we do. If we don't walk any differently from the world, we won't accomplish Christ's goals. If we live like the world, that

10

is like imitating the dead (Eph. 2:1-5), and that doesn't make sense.

Christians are like a new race. We have a new spiritual, incorruptible seed, and we must live a life-style that corresponds to it. We are new creations who have been suited for an eternal existence. Our new nature imputes Christ's righteousness and holiness to us. As a result we can discard our old life-style. Yet tragically the church does little to conform to the principles of Christ. Instead we often allow the world to shove us into its mold.

2. The people

The Greek word translated "Gentiles" (*ethnē*) is an ethnic term used in the New Testament to refer to non-Jewish races. However it also has a religious connotation, as in 1 Thessalonians 4:5, where Paul defines *ethnē* as those "who know not God." Thus it can refer to an ethnic group of non-Jews or to people who don't know God. Paul's point is we are not to live like people who don't know God.

3. The problem

The believers in Paul's day found it difficult to live differently than the unbelievers surrounding them. They were constantly subject to the vile habits and deeds of the pagans. We have the same problem today. The church in America has difficulty affecting people because our country is so affluent and is constantly inundated by the media's propagation of evil. Our problem isn't getting people in the world to live like Christians, but getting Christians to stop living like the world.

The Evils of Ephesus

Let's examine the pagan culture of Ephesus in Paul's day so that we can draw some parallels to our own day. Ephesus was one of the most dissolute and evil cities in Asia Minor. It served as a religious center, with multiple temples and idols. The worship in

11

Ephesus focused particularly on the goddess Diana (Gk., *Artemis*), often represented by an ugly multi-breasted beast.

The temple of Diana was one of the Seven Wonders of the World and served as more than a religious center. It was an art museum having one of the world's largest collections of art treasures. A quarter-mile-wide perimeter served as an asylum for criminals. The temple was the greatest bank in the world. A sacred temple was the perfect place for a bank in those days because the people feared reprisal from the gods for dishonesty. And it was also a place of business. Silversmiths made fortunes selling thousands of little idols. The people would put the idols in their homes, hang them around their necks, wear them on their wrists or ankles, and fasten them to the front of their chariots. Acts 19:23-41 records the events surrounding a revolt of silversmiths who feared Paul's preaching would ruin their business.

Diana was worshiped as a sex goddess. Pilgrims came by the thousands to worship there. (Where sex is the chief aspect of a religion, the religion will be extremely popular.) Scores of eunuchs, priestesses, temple prostitutes, singers, and dancers led the people in their worship, which was nothing more than great orgies. One writer said that the worship was a type of hysteria where the people, with shouts and music, worked themselves into frenzies of shameless sexual activity, including mutilation. Five centuries before Christ, Heraclitus, a Greek philosopher from Ephesus, criticized the lack of morals in his city and the temple (cf. *Diogenes Laertius: Lives of Emminent Philosophers*, 2 vols., R. D. Hicks, ed. [New York: Putnam, 1925], 2:409-10).

The church in Ephesus was like an island in a cesspool. What a vile, sinful world those early Christians had to live in! That's why Paul urged them to be different. Living the new life may be tough, but it is necessary.

4. The parallels

   a) 1 Peter 4:3—"The time past of our life may suffice us to have wrought the will of the Gentiles, when we walked in lasciviousness, lusts, excess of wine, revelings [wild parties], carousings, and abominable idolatries." Some of us may have done those things in the past, but now that we are Christians we must leave that life-style behind. Because of who we are in Christ and all that God desires of us, we are to be different from the world.

    b) 1 John 2:15, 17—"Love not the world, neither the things that are in the world. . . . The world passeth away, and the lust of it." The world is fading away, so we are warned to have no attachment to it. Our society is hostile to godliness because it is dominated by carnal ambition, pride, selfishness, greed, lust, and a desire for evil. Its opinions are wrong, its aims are selfish, its pleasures are sinful, its influence is destructive, its politics are corrupt, its honors are empty, its smiles are phony, and its love is fickle.

Paul wasn't just giving his own opinion, for he said, "This I say, therefore, and testify in the Lord" (Eph. 4:17). He was passing on information he had received from the Lord. Paul was promoting the divine life-style—God's standard, not his own.

Lesson

Having introduced verse 17, let's examine the contrast in verses 17-24 between the old walk and the new walk, or our old and new lifestyles. Paul described four characteristics of the old walk followed by four contrasting characteristics of the new walk.

I. THE OLD WALK (vv. 17*b*-19)

I believe the key issue in verses 17-24 is how people think. In verse 17 Paul says that unregenerate people live "in the vanity of their mind." He also speaks of understanding and ignorance (v. 18), learning and teaching (vv. 20-21), and the mind and truth (vv. 23-24). Proverbs 23:7 says, "As he thinketh in his heart, so is he." When Christians think differently from the world, they will act differently.

Salvation is first of all a change of mind. In verse 20 Paul says to believers, "Ye have not so learned Christ." Christianity is cognitive before it is experiential. We need to consider the gospel, believe its historic facts and spiritual truths, and then receive Christ as Savior and Lord. The first step in repentance is to think differently about our sin, about God, about Christ, and about our life than we used to think. The Greek word translated "repentance" means "to change one's mind." As it is used in the New Testament, it always refers to a change of purpose and a specific turning from sin.

Since an unbeliever thinks differently than a believer, let's look at four elements that characterize the thinking of an unbeliever.

A. Self-Centeredness (v. 17b)

"That ye henceforth walk not as other Gentiles walk, in the vanity of their mind."

Unbelievers value *their* mind, *their* thinking, *their* desires, and *their* whims. Whatever they think and whatever they want governs their behavior. Ephesians 2:3 says that when we were unbelievers "we all had our manner of life in times past in the lusts of our flesh, fulfilling the desires of the flesh and of the mind."

Paul characterized the self-centeredness of unbelievers as "vanity" (Gk., *mataios*, "that which is empty, futile, useless, or vain"). I believe "useless" is the best way to define it. Pagan thinking is useless because it accomplishes nothing.

Solomon was the wisest and richest man in the world. He had more women and prestige than any other man. Yet he summed up life this way, "Vanity of vanities . . . all is vanity. . . . This is also vanity and vexation of spirit" (Eccles. 1:2; 2:26).

It's tragic how people exhaust their money, their bodies, and their minds in attempts to find meaning in life, but never find it. Why? Because their thinking is empty and useless, accomplishing nothing. Jesus said, "Without me ye can do nothing" (John 15:5).

B. Ignorance (v. 18)

"Having the understanding darkened, being alienated from the life of God through the ignorance that is in them, because of the blindness of their heart."

It's difficult to face people who don't know Christ and tell them that they are ignorant. In an educated society such as ours, people will take that as an insult. No society in history has been more educated than ours, but as the apostle Paul said, people are "ever learning, and never able to come to the knowledge of the truth" (2 Tim. 3:7). Because of the Fall, we are born with a natural inability to understand the things of God. Romans 1:21-22 elaborates: "When they knew God, they glorified him not as God, neither were thankful, but became vain in their imaginations, and their foolish heart was darkened. Professing themselves to be wise, they became fools."

1. Darkened understanding

The Greek word translated "darkened" means "to make blind." In verse 18 this verb is in its perfect participle form, which implies it is something that happened in the past with continuing results in the present. Being darkened in their understanding is a continuing problem for unbelievers.

2. Alienation from God

When did man's understanding become darkened? Verse 18 says, "Being alienated from the life of God through the ignorance that is in them, because of the blindness [hardness] of their heart." A man's understanding is judicially darkened by a sovereign God when he willfully alienates himself from God, is willfully ignorant, and willfully hardens his heart. God affirms the choice that all men and women initially make.

a) God's confirmation

In reading about the Exodus of Israel we find that Pharaoh hardened his own heart several times. We

15

also read that God hardened Pharaoh's heart. If a person chooses a certain life-style and is confirmed in that life-style, God will judicially and sovereignly act to make that life-style permanent.

Since Jesus is the way, the truth, and the life (John 14:6), someone alienated from God cannot know the truth. In the same way that a corpse can't hear conversations in a mortuary, a spiritually dead individual cannot hear God. People alienated from God have no spiritual life in them.

As we noted in Romans 1, people refuse to honor God and therefore suffer the consequences (vv. 24, 26, 28). They choose the way to go, and God confirms them in their choice by giving them over to their evil desires.

b) Man's rejection

The Greek word translated "blindness" (*pōrōsis*) comes from the root *pōros*, which refers to a stone harder than marble. It was a medical term that referred to the callus that forms around a broken bone and the calcium deposits that can form in a joint and paralyze movement.

An unbeliever's life is like that—hard and without feeling toward God. Every time he takes another step of willful rejection, he pours more concrete upon his heart. The process is obvious—a man sins and feels guilt and remorse, sometimes very deeply, but tries to deny it. The more a person tries to eliminate his guilt by rationalization, self-justification, transferring the blame, or denial, the further away he pushes his guilt until he can't sense it anymore. That's when his conscience becomes seared, his heart petrified and insensitive, and his understanding permanently darkened.

John 12:37 says, "Though he [Jesus] had done so many miracles before them, yet they believed not on him." The people had sufficient information to be-

16

lieve in Jesus, but they willfully chose to be alienated from the life of God, to be ignorant, and to petrify their hearts with constant rejection. Verse 38 continues, "That the saying of Isaiah, the prophet, might be fulfilled, which he spoke, Lord, who hath believed our report? And to whom hath the arm of the Lord been revealed? Therefore, they could not believe because that Isaiah said again, He hath blinded their eyes, and hardened their heart; that they should not see with their eyes, nor understand with their heart, and be converted, and I should heal them" (vv. 38-40).

c) Satan's deception

Satan knows that Christianity and God's truth are issues of the mind. Second Corinthians 4:4 says, "The god of this age hath blinded the minds of them who believe not, lest the light of the glorious gospel of Christ, who is the image of God, should shine unto them." Satan blinds the mind. And as a man continues to willfully acquiesce to the activity of Satan, God will eventually blind his mind. Then that becomes his permanent state.

C. Shamelessness (v. 19*a*)

"Who, being past feeling."

When unbelievers continue in sin and turn themselves away from the life of God, they will become shameless—past any feeling. They become insensitive and apathetic, unconcerned about the consequences of their behavior. According to an old story, a Spartan youth stole a fox but ran into the man who owned the fox. Not wanting to betray the fact that he'd stolen the fox and that it was hidden under his tunic, the youth remained motionless while the fox tore at his midsection. Our society is standing motionless while sin tears it apart. People have become good at wearing masks. That gives rise to shameless behavior because all standards of morality are ignored.

D. Perversion (v. 19*b*)

"[They] have given themselves over unto lasciviousness, to work all uncleanness with greediness."

The Greek word translated "lasciviousness" (*aselgeia*) speaks of shameless wantonness and unblushing obscenity. It primarily refers to sexual obscenity. Basil, the fourth-century church Father, defined it as a disposition of the soul incapable of bearing the pain of discipline (cited by Richard C. Trench, *Synonyms of the New Testament* [Grand Rapids: Eerdmans, 1983 reprint], p. 56). Some bad men will try to hide their badness, but a man given over to *aselgeia* doesn't care whom he shocks or how indecent he is, just as long as he gratifies his own sick mind.

A person with a reprobate mind can't reason, be logical, or receive the truth. He continually gives himself to lasciviousness and does so without fear of shocking anyone. He may indulge in homosexuality, promiscuity, lying, cheating, and stealing.

"To work [Gk., *ergasia*, "business"] all uncleanness with greediness" implies that those people make a business out of evil and lust. That's certainly true of our society. There was a day when dirty business was hidden; now it's wholesale. Pornography, prostitution, X-rated films, suggestive TV programs, and other types of uncleanness form a large industry in our country.

Paul said such people pursue their evil with "greediness." The Greek word translated "greediness" means "a lawful desire for things that belong to others." Reprobates are after your purity, sanity, morality, and character. They want it all!

Conclusion

Paul looked at the evil pagan world and concluded that its self-centered, useless thinking leads to darkened understanding and hardheartedness. That in turn leads to insensitivity to sin and shameless behavior, which then leads to unblushing obscenity. Those who belong to the world make it their business to drag down others to their level.

But in Ephesians 4:20 Paul says, "Ye have not so learned [in] Christ." We're not to have any part of that old life-style. Instead we're to put off "the former manner of life" (v. 22) and "put on the new man, which after God is created in righteousness and true holiness" (v. 24).

Believers shouldn't be dabbling in any of the evils characteristic of unbelievers. We are to be a light on a hill, separate from the evil around us. We are to be different. A city that's set on a hill cannot be hidden. We must stand as salt and light. But if we are corrupted by the system, we become useless. Our blessed Lord Jesus Christ purchased us at the cost of His own life. He gave us a new nature that is holy, undefiled, and sanctified forever. He simply asks us to live up to what He has given us by discarding our old life-style and taking up our new one.

Focusing on the Facts

1. What change takes place when a person is saved (see p. 8)?
2. Since Christians are new creations, why do we continue to sin (see pp. 8-9)?
3. Does a Christian have two natures? Explain (see p. 9).
4. What did Paul say about the church in Ephesians 4:1-16 (see p. 10)?
5. In what ways are Christians different from unbelievers (see pp. 10-11)?
6. What is a major problem facing the church (see p. 11)?
7. Describe the culture the Ephesian believers had to live in (see pp. 11-12).
8. What is the key issue of Ephesians 4:17-21 (see p. 13)?
9. What is important to unbelievers (see p. 14)?
10. How did Paul characterize the self-centeredness of unbelievers (Eph. 4:17; see p. 14)?
11. What is a continual problem for unbelievers (see p. 15)?
12. In what way is an unbeliever's life like the callus that forms around a broken bone (see p. 16)?
13. How does Satan help unbelievers remain unbelievers (2 Cor. 4:4; see p. 17)?

14. Define lasciviousness. How does it characterize unbelievers (see p. 18)?

Pondering the Principles

1. Review Ephesians 4:1-16. Since the instruction Paul gives in verses 4:17-24 is a result of his previous discussion, answer the following questions about verses 1-16: According to verses 1-3, what is the worthy walk? How does Paul characterize the unity of the church in verses 4-6? Who are the gifted men that Christ gave to the church (v. 11)? What is their duty (v. 12)? According to verses 13-15, what results when we follow God's pattern for the church? Where does the power to do all that come from (v. 16)? Based on this brief study, what ought your commitment be to the church?

2. As believers we shouldn't participate in any of the evils in the world around us. Although we know that and probably don't exhibit a life characterized by a reprobate mind, shamelessness, or an ignorance of the truth, we must notice that the first characteristic is self-centeredness. Are there any aspects of your life that you are unwilling to give to God? A Christian ought to be fulfilling God's desires, not his own. Confess to God any areas of your life that you long to fulfill regardless of His will. Seek to replace those things with desires that will glorify God. As you do, you will find that God will give you a greater fulfillment than you've ever known before.

2
Off with the Old, On with the New—Part 2

Outline

Introduction

Review
I. The Old Walk (vv. 17b-19)
   A. Self-Centeredness (v. 17b)
   B. Ignorance (v. 18)
   C. Shamelessness (v. 19a)
   D. Perversion (v. 19b)

Lesson
   1. The characteristics of a reprobate mind
      a) "Lasciviousness"
         (1) Drunkenness
         (2) Sexual sin
      b) "Greediness"
   2. The choice of a reprobate mind
II. The New Walk (vv. 20-24)
   A. A Christ-Centered Life (vv. 20-21a)
   B. A Knowledge of the Truth (v. 21b)
   C. A Sensitivity to Sin (v. 22)
   D. A Renewed Mind (vv. 23-24)
      1. New thoughts (v. 23)
      2. New attitudes (v. 23)

Conclusion

Introduction

One of the great passages in the Bible, 1 John 5:4-5 is a fitting comparison to Ephesians 4:17-24: "Whatever is born of God overcometh the world; and this is the victory that overcometh the world, even our faith. Who is he that overcometh the world, but he that believeth that Jesus is the Son of God?" The Greek word translated "overcometh" (*nikē*) means "to conquer," "have victory," "be superior," or "overcome." Salvation transforms a loser into a winner and a victim into a victor. It allows us all to be overcomers.

In John 16:33 our Lord says, "In the world ye shall have tribulation: but be of good cheer; I have overcome the world." In becoming one with Jesus Christ, we become overcomers with Him. We rise above the world (1 John 5:4). We rise above death, saying with Paul, "O death, where is thy sting?" (1 Cor. 15:55). We rise above sin, for "sin shall not have dominion over you" (Rom. 6:14). And we also rise above Satan himself (1 John 4:4). Our citizenship is in heaven (Phil. 3:20). Therefore we are to live as heavenly citizens. As overcomers we are "risen with Christ" and are to "seek those things which are above" (Col. 3:1). Since we possess a new nature, we have the potential to adopt a new life-style. That's the essence of Paul's discussion in Ephesians 4:17-24.

Review

Whereas Ephesians 1-3 describes the new nature of the believer, chapters 4-6 describe how the new nature ought to manifest itself. Paul contrasted the old life-style and the new life-style, the old walk and the new walk. In 4:17 he says, "This I say, therefore, and testify in the Lord, that ye henceforth walk not as other Gentiles walk." Our new life-style is to be different from what it was before our salvation. In fact, God saves us so that we can be different. According to Ephesians 2:10 we are "created in Christ Jesus unto good works, which God hath before ordained that we should walk in them." In 2 Corinthians 5:17 Paul says, "If any man be in Christ, he is a new creation; old things are passed away; behold, all things are become new." Although we are overcomers, 1 John 5:19 says, "The whole world lieth in wickedness." The world is coddled by Satan, but we have risen above it into the very presence of God. We aren't like "Gentiles who know not God" (1 Thess. 4:5). When we come to Jesus Christ we are transformed, and our life-style is to match our new nature.

The key to our new nature is the way we think. That's why Ephesians 4:23 says, "Be renewed in the spirit of your mind." We are not to think the way we did before we knew Christ.

Before we look at the walk of the new man, let's review the characteristics of the old walk.

I. THE OLD WALK (vv. 17b-19; see pp. 13-19)

Ephesians 2:1-3 informs us that sinners walk according to the world, the flesh, and the devil. In Ephesians 4:17-19 Paul shows the results of that kind of walk by delineating four characteristics of pagan thinking and life-style.

A. Self-Centeredness (v. 17b; see p. 14)

"Ye henceforth walk not as other Gentiles walk, in the vanity of their mind."

B. Ignorance (v. 18; see pp. 15-17)

"Having the understanding darkened, being alienated from the life of God through the ignorance that is in them, because of the blindness [hardness] of their heart."

C. Shamelessness (v. 19a; see p. 17)

"Who, being past feeling."

D. Perversion (v. 19b; see p. 18)

"[They] have given themselves over unto lasciviousness, to work all uncleanness with greediness."

Lesson

1. The characteristics of a reprobate mind

   a) "Lasciviousness"

   The Greek word translated "lasciviousness" (*aselgeia*) refers to the person who is so dominated by sin that he doesn't care what people say or think. He is not shocked by his own sin; he has no sense of decency or shame.

   Aselgeia is rarely used alone in the New Testament. It is usually connected with the following:

   (1) Drunkenness

   In Romans 13:13, Galatians 5:19-21, and 1 Peter 4:3 *aselgeia* is listed with a particular type of drunkenness referred to as "reveling" (Gk., *kōmos*). Originally *kōmos* referred to a band of friends who accompanied a victor home from the games. Usually they got drunk along the way. Eventually *kōmos* came to mean "brawling in drunkenness." When connected with *aselgeia*, it referred to a person whose self-indulgence and lack of restraint gave way to ribald drunkenness.

   (2) Sexual sin

   In Mark 7:22, 2 Corinthians 12:21, Galatians 5:19, and 2 Peter 2:18 *aselgeia* is mentioned with sexual sin. A lascivious person has no more shame than an animal gratifying his or her sexual desire.

   b) "Greediness"

   In Mark 7:22, 2 Peter 2:2-3, and our present text, Ephesians 4:19, *aselgeia* is used with *pleonexia*, which is translated "greediness." It is not some isolated inner attitude but an uncontrollable vice.

Unbelievers are characterized by lasciviousness, which can involve drunkenness, sexual indecency, and uncontrollable lust. While it is true that most unbelievers don't live to that extreme, they don't have the resources to restrain themselves. Only by the grace of God exhibited in the world through the preserving influence of the Holy Spirit and the church does anyone avoid such depths of evil.

(1) Romans 1:29—Here *pleonexia* reveals the sin of the godless as they turn their backs on God to fulfill their desires.

(2) Luke 12:15—Greediness also characterizes the person who evaluates life only in material terms.

(3) 1 Thessalonians 2:5—*Pleonexia* describes those who take advantage of others (cf. 4:6).

(4) Colossians 3:5—Here *pleonexia* is identified with idolatry because it is the worship of things rather than the true God.

In many passages, including Ephesians 4:19, *pleonexia* is connected with sexual evil. It is the desire to have the illicit and forbidden and wanting it so badly that a person is willing to destroy anyone or anything in his way. There are many people like that in our society. And there will be more: 2 Timothy 3:13 says, "Evil men and seducers shall become worse and worse." As we move closer to the time of our Lord's return, those kind of people will inundate society.

2. The choice of a reprobate mind

How do people become so degenerate? Ephesians 4:19 says they "have given themselves over" to lasciviousness. They make a constant, willful choice. And a choice made often becomes a habit. One's habits reap one's personality, one's personality reaps one's character, and one's character reaps one's destiny. It all begins with a series of choices. You cannot blame sin on anyone but yourself.

Understanding the Criminal Mind

For years criminal behavior was believed to result from environmental factors such as where a person lived or how he was treated by his parents. But that perspective was challenged by two researchers, Samuel Yochelson and Stanton Samenow, in *The Criminal Personality* (New York: Jason Aronsen, 1976, 1977, 1986). This three-volume work, the result of years of clinical study of criminals, is highly regarded by those in law enforcement who analyze criminal behavior.

The thesis of the study is that criminal behavior is the result of warped thinking processes. In fact, three sections of volume one (more than 200 pages) are devoted to "thinking errors characteristic of the criminal." The researchers wrote, "Abandoning the search for causation and deciding not to work with feelings, we probed the criminal patterns of thought" (p. 52). They concluded, "It is remarkable that the criminal often derives as great an impact from his activities during nonarrestable phases as he does from crime. . . . The criminal's thinking patterns operate everywhere; they are not restricted to crime" (p. 53). The thinking process of the criminal mind is out of whack. Romans 1:28 calls it "a reprobate mind." The problem is in the criminal's mind, not his environment.

In endeavoring to explain the criminal mind, the researchers realized that common psychological and sociological explanations were unsatisfactory: "The idea that a man becomes a criminal because he is corrupted by his environment has proved to be too [weak] an explanation. . . . We have indicated that criminals come from a broad spectrum of homes, both disadvantaged and privileged. Within the same neighborhood, some are violators, and most are not. It is not the environment that turns a man into a criminal. Rather, it is a series of choices that he makes starting at a very early age" (pp. 104, 247).

They went on to conclude, "Perhaps most important is that [our studies have] demonstrated that a criminal is not a victim of circumstances. He makes choices early in life, regardless of his socioeconomic status, race, or parents' child-rearing practices. . . . Changing the environment does not change the man" (p. 249).

The Greek word translated "work" in Ephesians 4:19 (*ergasia*) is sometimes used to refer to a business. People are so vile that they turn their sin into a business. That makes sense because men are greedy.

Our X-Rated Economy

Forbes magazine ([Sept. 18, 1978] :81-92) ran a lead article entitled "The X-Rated Economy," by James Cook. He began by stating the obvious—that pornography is no longer illegal. Neither is the market confined to perverts or other emotional cripples. Instead, middle class people make up the largest part of pornography's market. "In an increasingly . . . permissive society, those who enjoy pornography are free to revel in it" (p. 81).

Cook went on to say that according to the California Department of Justice, the nation's pornographers do more than $4 billion of business a year—more than the combined incomes of the often supportive movie and music industries. Other estimates place the total pornographic business—including a large segment of the burgeoning home video market—at three times that much. The article said that skin magazines circulate 16 million copies a month and generate nearly $500 million a year in revenue. Adult films are seen by two million people per week at $3.50 per ticket, grossing more than 365 million dollars. (Remember, this article was written in 1978, so all these figures are much higher today.) Another $100 million is spent on sex toys. But the biggest market of all, Cook tells us, is "adult" bookstores. Some bookstores in New York take in $10,000 a day. The Los Angeles Police Department estimates that $125 million annually is spent in bookstores throughout the city.

Pornography is big business, but it is part of the old life. The apostle Paul rightly instructed us not to walk as unbelievers (Eph. 4:17). Their life-style is not to be ours.

Examine Yourself!

Are you still hanging onto the life-style you followed before you became a Christian? James 4:4 says, "Ye adulterers and adulteresses, know ye not that the friendship of the world is enmity with

God? Whosoever, therefore, will be a friend of the world is the ene-
my of God." I believe that if you didn't make a conscious effort to
cut yourself off from the system of this world when you came to
Christ, you have reason to question whether your salvation was
genuine.

First John 2:15 says, "Love not the world, neither the things that
are in the world. If any man love the world, the love of the Father is
not in him." When a person becomes a Christian, he desires to cut
himself off from the world. Although the world continues to tempt
us from time to time, we must forsake the devil's evil system.

An immoral, ungodly person who supposedly accepts Jesus but
never changes his life-style is not a Christian. To say that a person
can come to Christ without making a break from the world is a lie.
That kind of thinking will send people down the broad road to de-
struction rather than down the narrow way to salvation (Matt.
7:13-14). There must be a change of life-style!

People in the world live in ignorance, following their own musings
without decency in a greedy quest to fulfill their lusts (Eph. 4:17-
19). But when a person comes to Jesus Christ, he recognizes what
his life has been and knows it can now be different. It's not an easy
life—that's why Paul commanded us not to live as we did before
we came to Christ (Eph. 4:17). But we can live God's way because
we have a new nature.

Is Repentance Necessary for Salvation?

On the day of Pentecost, the apostle Peter preached a powerful sermon that tremendously affected the people who heard it. Acts 2:37
says, "When they heard this, they were pricked in their heart, and
said unto Peter and to the rest of the apostles, Men and brethren,
what shall we do?" The people realized that they were in a terrible
condition and that they needed to do something different to get
out of it.

The first thing Peter said they needed to do was "repent" (v. 38).
No one can come to Jesus Christ unless he repents. Jesus began His
ministry proclaiming, "Repent; for the kingdom of heaven is at
hand" (Matt. 4:17). The apostle Paul preached "repentance toward

28

God, and faith toward our Lord Jesus Christ" (Acts 20:21). Peter went on to say, "Be baptized, every one of you, in the name of Jesus Christ for the remission of sins" (Acts 2:38). Repentance is a conscious choice to turn from the world, sin, and evil. It is crucial!

Verse 40 continues, "With many other words did [Peter] testify and exhort, saying, Save yourselves from this crooked generation." Peter exhorted the people to cut themselves off from the world, change their life-styles, turn their backs on their sinfulness, and live holy lives. You can't be saved if you don't repent of your sin and make a break with the world.

If you came to Jesus Christ thinking all you had to do was believe, without confessing your sin or being willing to cut yourself off from this evil world, you missed the point of salvation. Many people's lives haven't changed at all since they supposedly believed in Christ. For example, some used to act immorally and still act immorally. Some committed adultery and continue to commit adultery. And others committed fornication and still commit fornication. Yet according to 1 Corinthians 6:9-10, fornicators and adulterers will not inherit the kingdom of God. If you are really saved, you will make a conscious attempt to break away from the things of the world, so don't go back to them.

II. THE NEW WALK (vv. 20-24)

When we became Christians God gave us a different kind of mind. Peter called it a pure mind (2 Pet. 3:1). Paul said to be "transformed by the renewing of your mind" (Rom. 12:2). What are the characteristics of the believer's mind?

A. A Christ-Centered Life (vv. 20-21a)

"Ye have not so learned [from] Christ, if so be that ye have heard him."

We are no longer controlled by a self-centered mind; we learn from Christ. Christ acts through us, loves through us, feels through us, and serves through us. The lives we live are not ours but Christ living in us (Gal. 2:20). Philippians 2:5 says, "Let this mind be in you, which was also in Christ Jesus." Christ Himself said, "Ye should do as I have done

29

to you" (John 13:15). We are to love as Christ has loved us (Eph. 5:2). First John 2:6 says, "He that saith he abideth in him [Christ] ought himself also so to walk, even as he walked." An unsaved person walks in the vanity of his own mind, but a saved person walks according to the mind of Christ.

The Greek word translated "learned" (*manthanō*) means "to learn by inquiry." As a person inquires about Jesus Christ and discovers the reality of who He is and commits his life to Him, Christ begins to think for him. Paul said, "Nevertheless I live; yet not I, but Christ liveth in me" (Gal. 2:20).

God has a plan for the universe, and as long as Christ is working in us, He is working out a part of that plan through us. Paul noted that He "is able to do exceedingly abundantly above all that we ask or think, according to the power that worketh in us" (Eph. 3:20). Every day is a fantastic adventure for the Christian because we are in the middle of God's unfolding plan for the ages.

B. A Knowledge of the Truth (v. 21*b*)

"[You] have been taught by him, as the truth is in Jesus."

When you give your life to Christ you are saying to Him, "You are the ruler of all. I acknowledge that You are Lord." You can't become a Christian without somehow acknowledging the lordship of Christ. When you give Him your life, you come under the truth. In 2 Corinthians 11:10 Paul says, "The truth of Christ is in me." First John 5:20-21 says, "We know that the Son of God is come, and hath given us an understanding, that we may know him that is true; and we are in him that is true, even in his Son Jesus Christ. This is the true God, and eternal life. Little children, keep yourselves from idols."

When we come to know Christ, we come to know the truth about God, man, sin, creation, death, life, history, relationships, salvation, happiness, purpose, meaning, heaven, hell, faith, and grace.

C. A Sensitivity to Sin (v. 22)

"Put off concerning the former manner of life the old man, which is corrupt according to the deceitful lusts."

Christians know what it means to be corrupt and to see the result of lust. That's because we are sensitive to sin. Jesus said, "Blessed are they that mourn; for they shall be comforted" (Matt. 5:4). True subjects of the kingdom mourn over their sin. First John 1:8-10 says, "If we say that we have no sin, we deceive ourselves, and the truth is not in us. If we confess our sins, he is faithful and just to forgive our sins, and to cleanse us from all unrighteousness. If we say that we have not sinned, we make him a liar, and his word is not in us." A true Christian will acknowledge his sin because he is sensitive to it.

In Romans 7 we learn that Paul before his conversion was never as sensitive to sin as he was after he became a Christian. In verse 24 he says, "Oh, wretched man that I am! Who shall deliver me from the body of this death?" He wasn't expressing an isolated experience but a way of life—a deep sensitivity to his own sinfulness.

D. A Renewed Mind (vv. 23-24)

1. New thoughts (v. 23)

"Be renewed in the spirit of your mind."

The Greek word translated "renewed" (*ananeoō*) is used only here in the New Testament. It means "to create again" or "make new." When you become a Christian, God gives you a new mind, but you must fill it with new thoughts. A baby is born with a fresh, new mind, and then impressions are made on it that determine the course of his life. The same thing is true of a Christian. You enter into God's kingdom and you receive a fresh, new mind. You then need to build the right thoughts into your new mind. That's why Philippians 4:8 says, "Whatever things are true, whatever things are honest, whatever things are just, whatever things are pure,

31

whatever things are lovely, whatever things are of good report; if there be any virtue, and if there be any praise, think on these things." We have a renewed mind, not a reprobate mind.

2. New attitudes (v. 24)

"Put on the new man, which after God is created in righteousness and true holiness."

Instead of having a reprobate, vile, lascivious, greedy, unclean mind, we have a mind filled with righteousness and holiness. That naturally characterizes the way we live.

Conclusion

We're to "put off . . . the old man" (v. 22) and "put on the new man" (v. 24). When you came to Christ you acknowledged that you were a sinner and chose to forsake your sin and the evil things of this world. But Satan will dangle the temptations of the world and its sin in front of you to tempt you to return to it. So Paul warned us not to return to the world but to put it off and instead put on righteousness and true holiness.

That's not something you do once; it's something you do every day. But how? Note the following resources. Second Timothy 3:16 says, "All scripture is given by inspiration of God, and is profitable for doctrine, for reproof, for correction." If you want to live correctly, expose yourself to the Word of God. It will help you deal with the traces of the world still present in your life. Also take advantage of prayer. First John 1:9 says that if we confess our sins, we will be forgiven. Let the Word of God expose your sin, and let God through prayer cleanse you from it.

Focusing on the Facts

1. In what sense is a Christian an overcomer (see p. 22)?
2. With what two words is *aselgeia* often connected? Explain each (see p. 24).

3. What word is *aselgeia* connected with in Ephesians 4:19? Define (see pp. 24-25).
4. How do people become reprobate (see p. 25)?
5. What conclusions about the criminal personality did Yochelson and Samenow come to in their book (see p. 26)?
6. What current example from our society shows that people turn uncleanness into a business (see p. 27)?
7. What kind of thinking about the nature of salvation can lead people down the wrong road (see p. 28)?
8. When the people who heard Peter's sermon on the Day of Pentecost asked what they should do, what did Peter say? Explain (Acts 2:38; see pp. 28-29).
9. What kind of mind is a Christian to have (see p. 29)?
10. What are you saying to Christ when you give your life to Him (see p. 30)?
11. Why do true subjects of God's kingdom mourn over their sin (see p. 31)?
12. What two resources will help you put on righteousness and holiness each day (see p. 32)?

Pondering the Principles

1. Throughout the centuries, athletes have endured grueling training to gain victory and the accompanying spoils, only to find that victory itself is often elusive. However, Christians, as overcomers, have complete certainty about the ultimate victory, which is eternal life with Jesus Christ (1 John 5:1-5, 11-13). Look up the following verses, and note how you can have victory over Satan (Matt. 4:1-11), death (John 5:24; 1 Cor. 15:54-57), and the world (1 John 5:4).

2. Review the section on the new walk (pp. 29-32). What are the four characteristics of the believer's mind? Note that you don't have to acquire those characteristics; they already are yours if you are a believer. Unfortunately our practice sometimes doesn't match our position in Christ. According to the conclusion of this chapter, what two things must you do to make those four characteristics a reality in your life? Plan to implement the two resources at your disposal on a daily basis.

3
Principles of New Life

Outline

Introduction and Review
 I. Lying Versus Telling the Truth (v. 25)
   A. The World of Lies
     1. The future of liars
     2. The father of lies
   B. The World of Truth
     1. The enemy of truth
     2. The importance of truth
 II. Unrighteous Anger Versus Righteous Anger (vv. 26-27)
   A. The Command (v. 26*a*)
     1. Anger defined
     2. Anger discussed
       a) Unrighteous anger
       b) Righteous anger
   B. The Commitment (vv. 26*b*-27)
     1. To deal with sin (v. 26*b*)
     2. To deal with Satan (v. 27)
 III. Stealing Versus Sharing (v. 28)
   A. A Scriptural Overview on Stealing
     1. Non-payment of debts (Ps. 37:21)
     2. Falsifying account books (Luke 16:1-13)
     3. Cheating on taxes (Matt. 22:17-22)
     4. Using improper measurements (Amos 8:5; Hos. 12:7)
     5. Not paying a fair wage (James 5:4)
   B. A Scriptural Overview on Working
 IV. Corrupt Speech Versus Edifying Speech (vv. 29-30)
   A. The Contrast (v. 29)
     1. The uselessness of corrupt speech
       a) The elimination of rotten words
       b) The source of rotten words

Introduction and Review

Ephesians 4:25-32 says, "Putting away lying, speak every man truth with his neighbor; for we are members one of another. Be ye angry, and sin not; let not the sun go down upon your wrath; neither give place to the devil. Let him that stole steal no more but, rather, let him labor, working with his hands the thing which is good, that he may have to give to him that needeth. Let no corrupt communication proceed out of your mouth, but that which is good to the use of edifying, that it may minister grace unto the hearers. And grieve not the Holy Spirit of God, by whom ye are sealed unto the day of redemption. Let all bitterness, and wrath, and anger, and clamor, and evil speaking, be put away from you, with all malice; and be ye kind one to another, tenderhearted, forgiving one another, even as God, for Christ's sake, hath forgiven you."

In Ephesians 4:17-24 the apostle Paul makes the point that Christians are to be different. We are not to walk as unbelievers walk, that is, in blindness, darkness, and hardness of their hearts (vv. 17-18). They tend to be insensitive, immoral, unclean, and greedy (v. 19), but we are to be like Christ. We are to put off the old man (v. 22) and put on the new man (v. 24). We are to exchange our old lifestyle for a new one. Verses 25-32 list specific categories in which the exchanges are to occur.

I. LYING VERSUS TELLING THE TRUTH (v. 25)

"Putting away lying, speak every man truth with his neighbor; for we are members one of another."

The Greek word translated "put away" (*apotithēmi*) speaks of throwing something off like an old coat. It is used in Acts 7:58 when the Jewish leaders threw their coats at Paul's feet before they stoned Stephen. The phrase "speak every man truth to his neighbor" is a quotation from Zechariah 8:16. Paul related the Old Testament to this important truth.

A. The World of Lies

1. The future of liars

Revelation 21:8 says, "The fearful, and unbelieving, and the abominable, and murderers, and fornicators, and sorcerers, and idolaters, and all liars, shall have their part in the lake which burneth with fire and brimstone." One thing is certain: liars will go to hell. Conversely, those who go to heaven are not liars. Lying is not characteristic of a believer. There may be times when a believer lies, but if a person continually lies, there is no basis for believing he is a Christian.

2. The father of lies

John 8:44 tells us that the devil is a liar and the father of all lies. Therefore habitual liars give indication of having the devil as their father and hell as their destiny. No matter what they may claim or how religious they may be, they won't be a part of God's kingdom because liars don't go to heaven. Instead, believers forsake lying and speak the truth.

Lying is characteristic of our world. Lawyers, doctors, teachers, preachers, salesmen, secretaries, bosses, advertisers, and politicians all lie. The system operates on what's expedient, and lying is expedient—but only for the moment.

People lie because their nature is depraved. Their father is the devil, who developed a world system based on lies. Religious systems apart from Christianity are for the most part lies mixed with shades of truth. Satan lies about life, death, God, Christ, the Holy Spirit, the Bible, heaven, hell, good, and evil. The entire world system—religious, economic, and governmental—is based on lies.

B. The World of Truth

When God comes into a person's life, the truth becomes important to him. Romans 3:4 says, "Let God be true, but every man a liar." Jesus said, "I am the way, the truth, and the life" (John 14:6). The Holy Spirit, who takes up residence in the believer's life, is called "the Spirit of truth," who guides us into all truth (John 16:13). Of God's Word Jesus said, "Thy word is truth" (John 17:17). When a person becomes a believer he leaves the domain of lies and enters the realm of truth. He is now redeemed by the true Messiah and indwelt by the true Spirit. He knows the true God, possesses the true Word, and lives a true life. Whenever a believer speaks, he should be speaking the truth (Eph. 4:15).

1. The enemy of truth

A Christian should not tell any kind of lie. The most familiar kind of lie is saying something that isn't true. But there are other kinds, such as exaggeration. A certain Christian man had a powerful testimony, but one day he stopped reciting it. When asked why, he said that through the years he had embellished it so much he had forgotten what was true and what he'd made up.

Cheating in school, in business, at work, and on your taxes is a form of lying. So is betraying a confidence, flattery, making excuses, and remaining silent when the truth should be spoken. There's no place for lying in the Christian life. One of the Ten Commandments is "Thou shalt not bear false witness" (Ex. 20:16). We are to tell the truth.

However, beware of psychological "honesty" that is used in sensitivity training. One of the exercises used in that form of training requires one person to tell another what he doesn't like about him. If you are a Christian and you feel hatred toward someone, you don't need to express it. Instead you need to go to God and deal with the hate in your heart, asking Him to replace it with love. We are to eliminate lying from all our relationships, but that doesn't give us license to express our hatred.

2. The importance of truth

Why is it important to tell the truth? Ephesians 4:25 says, "We are members one of another." Ephesians is a book about the Body of Christ and the unity of the church. When we don't speak the truth with each other, we harm our fellowship. For example, what would happen if your brain told you that cold was hot and hot was cold? When you took a shower you'd either freeze to death or scald yourself! If your eye decided to send false signals to your brain, a dangerous curve in the highway might appear straight and you would crash. You depend on the honesty of your nervous system and of every organ in your body. God has built into your body a system that senses pain and fights disease. Accurate signals are what allow our bodies to function.

The Body of Christ can't function with any less than that. We cannot shade the truth with others and expect the church to function properly. How can we minister to each other, bear each other's burdens, care for each other, love each other, build up each other, teach each other, and pray for each other if we do not know what is going on in each others' lives? Be honest, "speaking the truth in love" (Eph. 4:15).

II. UNRIGHTEOUS ANGER VERSUS RIGHTEOUS ANGER (vv. 26-27)

A. The Command (v. 26a)

"Be ye angry, and sin not."

1. Anger defined

   Three Greek words are often translated "anger": *thumos, parorgismos,* and *orgē.*

   a) *Thumos* refers to a fury out of control. It sometimes refers to something that has gone up in smoke.

   b) *Parorgismos* is an internal seething, a fuming resentment that most often arises out of jealousy.

   c) *Orgē* refers to anger based on a settled conviction. People have certain priorities to which they are committed, and when something violates those priorities, they respond accordingly. For example, you love your children with all your heart, but if someone hurts them you become angry.

   You can be angry and sin or be angry and not sin. Your motive is the issue.

2. Anger discussed

   a) Unrighteous anger

   Thumos should never characterize a Christian. In the New Testament it refers to unregenerate men or to someone engaging in sin. It is also used of Satan (Rev. 12:12) and God's ultimate wrath upon sinners (Rom. 2:8). Only God can go to the extreme end of anger and still be righteous, because He is always under control. But to us *thumos* is unrighteous because we are unable to control it.

   b) Righteous anger

   Sometimes *parorgismos* and *orgē* can rightfully characterize a Christian as long as the anger is not caused by selfish motives. We can be angry over what grieves God and hinders His causes. But we are not to be so angry that we sin. Don't be angry for your own causes. Don't get angry when people offend you. Don't let your anger degenerate into personal resentment, bitterness, sullenness, or moodiness.

That is forbidden. The only justifiable anger is anger that defends the great, glorious, and holy nature of our God.

(1) Exemplified by Jesus

In John 2:13-17 we see the majestic indignation of Christ on display as He cleansed the Temple. God's holiness was at stake, so Jesus took decisive action against the unrighteousness He found in the Temple.

John 11:33 says Jesus "groaned in the spirit, and was troubled." It's quite possible that Jesus was experiencing inner fury over the consequences of the Fall when He saw that His friend Lazarus was dead. Seeing Lazarus may have brought to mind the terrible things He would endure on the cross when He bore the sins of the world in His own body. Jesus was angry about sin—and He had a right to be.

(2) Exemplified by Paul

The apostle Paul became angry with the Corinthians because they didn't get angry about sin in their congregation (1 Cor. 5:1-2). They tolerated incest in their fellowship and didn't become angry about it when they should have.

In 1 Timothy 1:20 Paul apparently was so angry at Hymenaeus and Alexander that he threw them out of the church and delivered them to Satan.

(3) Exemplified by the psalmists

Psalm 97:10 says, "Ye who love the Lord, hate evil." David said, "Zeal of thine house hath eaten me up; and the reproaches of those who reproached thee are fallen upon me" (Ps. 69:9).

What people do to God's name ought to infuriate you. But according to Matthew 5:21-22 the wrong kind of anger is the first step toward murder. I admit

41

to getting angry sometimes. I hope I never get angry about what happens to me but only about abuse of God's holy name. Anger that is selfish, passionate, undisciplined, and uncontrolled is sinful, useless, and hurtful. It must be banished from the Christian life. But the disciplined anger that seeks the righteousness of God is pure, selfless, and dynamic. We ought to be angry about the sin in the world and in the church. But we can't let that anger degenerate into sin. That's why Paul said, "Be ye angry, and sin not" (Eph. 4:26).

B. The Commitment (vv. 26b-27)

1. To deal with sin (v. 26b)

"Let not the sun go down upon your wrath."

That refers to the wrong kind of anger. If our anger has become sin, we are to deal with it now and not sleep on it. The New Testament continually exhorts us to face sin and deal with it now by confessing and repenting of it. If we don't and instead harbor an unforgiving spirit, Satan will "get an advantage of us" (2 Cor. 2:11).

2. To deal with Satan (v. 27)

"Neither give place to the devil."

The Greek word translated "devil" (*diabolos*) means "slanderer." Anger will inevitably lead to slander—either in speech or thoughts. That gives a place to the slander. As John 8:44 indicates, when a person constantly lies he gives evidence that his father is the devil. Similarly, people who are continually angry reveal that they too belong to him.

III. STEALING VERSUS SHARING (v. 28)

"Let him that stole steal no more but, rather, let him labor, working with his hands the thing which is good, that he may have to give to him that needeth."

Theft is a common problem in our world. Shoplifting has become such a problem that a significant percentage of the cost of items in the store covers the amount lost from stolen goods. Whether grand theft or petty theft, robbing from the store or stealing money from a rich man or a family member, it is all stealing.

A. A Scriptural Overview on Stealing

The Bible discusses many different kinds of stealing.

1. Nonpayment of debts (Ps. 37:21)

2. Falsifying account books (Luke 16:1-13)

3. Cheating on taxes (Matt. 22:17-22)

4. Using improper measurements (Amos 8:5; Hos. 12:7)

5. Not paying a fair wage (James 5:4)

For those who steal, 1 Corinthians 6:9-10 offers this warning: "Know ye not that the unrighteous shall not inherit the kingdom of God? Be not deceived: neither fornicators, nor idolaters, nor adulterers, nor effeminate, nor abusers of themselves with mankind, *nor thieves*, nor covetous, nor drunkards, nor revilers, nor extortioners, shall inherit the kingdom of God" (emphasis added).

B. A Scriptural Overview on Working

Ephesians 4:28 says, "Rather, let him labor, working with his hands the thing which is good, that he may have to give to him that needeth." The Greek word translated "labor" refers to hard, manual labor. Hard work is honorable.

1. Exodus 20:9—"Six days shalt thou labor and do all thy work."

2. 2 Thessalonians 3:10-11—"This we commanded you, that if any would not work, neither should he eat. For we hear that there are some who walk among you disorderly, working not at all but are busybodies."

3. 1 Timothy 5:8—"If any provide not for his own, and specially for those of his own house, he hath denied the faith, and is worse than an infidel."

As Christians we should work hard so that we have enough to give to those in need, not so that we will have more of what we don't need. The worldly approach to wealth is to hoard what we acquire. But the New Testament principle is to work hard so that we might do good and give to those who have needs.

In Luke 14:13-14 our Lord says, "When thou givest a feast, call the poor, the maimed, the lame, the blind, and thou shalt be blessed; for they cannot recompense thee." In Acts 20:33-34 Paul says, "I have coveted no man's silver, or gold, or apparel. Yea, ye yourselves know that these hands have ministered unto my necessities, and to them that were with me." Paul took care of his own needs and the needs of those who traveled with him.

IV. CORRUPT SPEECH VERSUS EDIFYING SPEECH (vv. 29-30)

A. The Contrast (v. 29)

"Let no corrupt communication proceed out of your mouth, but that which is good to the use of edifying, that it may minister grace unto the hearers."

1. The uselessness of corrupt speech

The Greek word translated "corrupt" (*sapros*) means "rotten." It refers to something that is worthless, useless, or diseased. Rotten fruit smells terrible and is worthless. You don't want to get near it, let alone eat it. The same thing is true of rotten language. Whether it is off-color jokes, profanity, dirty stories, or crude speech, in no way should it characterize a Christian.

a) The elimination of rotten words

(1) Psalm 141:3—"Set a watch, O Lord, before my mouth; keep the door of my lips." If Jesus Christ is the doorkeeper of your lips, He will be the one to determine what comes out of them.

(2) Colossians 3:8—"Put off all these: anger, wrath, malice, blasphemy, filthy communication out of your mouth."

(3) Ephesians 5:3-4—"Fornication, and all uncleanness, or covetousness, let it not be once named among you, as becometh saints; neither filthiness, nor foolish talking."

b) The source of rotten words

(1) Matthew 12:34—Jesus said, "Out of the abundance of the heart the mouth speaketh." You can tell a lot about a person's heart by what comes out of his mouth.

(2) Romans 3:9-14—In Paul's discussion of the depravity of mankind, he shows how depravity begins inside us and proceeds out of our mouths.

2. The benefits of good speech

Ephesians 4:29 contains three features of the speech of the new man.

a) It is edifying

If you allow the Lord to keep watch over your lips, whatever you say should build up others. You should encourage and strengthen others spiritually. Is that what happens when you talk with people? Do they go away built up in Jesus Christ? Mothers, when you are with your children throughout the day, do your words to them build them up? Fathers, when you take your children out for the day, are your conversations with them edifying and encouraging?

b) It is necessary

In verse 29 the phrase "to the use" means "as it fits the need." When I was growing up, whenever I'd say to my mom, "Do you know what So-and-so did?" she would respond, "Is that necessary?" Often

45

what I wanted to say was interesting, but it certainly wasn't necessary.

c) It is gracious

Verse 29 also tells us our speech should "minister grace to the hearers." Do your words bless those who hear them? Is there graciousness in what you say?

(1) Luke 4:22—"All bore [Jesus] witness, and wondered at the gracious words which proceeded out of his mouth."

(2) Colossians 3:16—"Let the word of Christ dwell in you richly . . . singing with grace in your hearts to the Lord." If you allow the Lord to set a watch over your tongue, and His Word dwells in you, your words will be the gracious words of Christ.

(3) Colossians 4:6—"Let your speech be always with grace, seasoned with salt." Do your words act as salt and retard the corruption in the world, or do they contribute to it?

B. The Command (v. 30)

"Grieve not the Holy Spirit of God, by whom ye are sealed unto the day of redemption."

"Grieve" is another word for "sadden." The Holy Spirit grieves when believers don't exchange their old life-style for the new one. He is grieved when believers lie and obscure the truth, when they're angry and unforgiving, when they steal and refuse to share, and when they speak corruptly and lack a spirit of graciousness.

When you were saved, the Spirit of God put a seal on you, declaring that you belong to God forever. Since the Spirit of God has been gracious enough to give you eternal salvation, seal you forever, and keep your salvation secure until the day of redemption, how could you willfully grieve Him? He has done so much for us that in our gratitude we ought not to grieve Him.

V. NATURAL VICES VERSUS SUPERNATURAL GRACES (vv. 31-32)

A. The Natural Vices (v. 31)

"Let all bitterness, and wrath, and anger, and clamor, and evil speaking, be put away from you, with all malice."

1. "Bitterness"—smoldering resentment that results in a brooding, grudging, unforgiving spirit.

2. "Wrath"—a wild rage arising from selfishness.

3. "Anger"—a settled, internal resentment.

4. "Clamor"—violent public outbursts.

5. "Evil speaking"—slander.

Each of those vices illustrates how not to relate to others. Christians must not be bitter, wrathful, resentful, violent, or slanderous. We must get rid of those attitudes. In fact Paul tells us to put away "all malice." The Greek word translated "malice" (*kakia*) refers to evil in general. We need to eliminate all forms of evil from our relationships.

B. The Supernatural Graces (v. 32)

"Be ye kind one to another, tenderhearted, forgiving one another, even as God, for Christ's sake, hath forgiven you."

God was kind and tenderhearted toward you, forgiving you even when you didn't deserve it. If you base your attitude toward people on what they deserve, you've missed the point. Don't yell at people, slander them, or get angry at them, even if they deserve it. Those who exemplify God's character are loving, kind, tender, and forgiving. That's the kind of attitude God expects from those who are new creations in Christ.

Conclusion

If Christians never lied but always spoke the truth, never became angry in a sinful way but always acted in love, never stole but always shared, never spoke in a coarse manner but always spoke edifying words, never were bitter, wrathful, resentful, violent, or slanderous but were always characterized by kindness, tenderheartedness, and forgiveness, don't you think the world would pay more attention to our message?

Examine yourself: Do you speak the truth? Do you have control over your anger so that it operates only in righteousness? Do you share your resources with others? Do you speak graciously? Are you kind, tenderhearted, and forgiving? If you are a new man or woman in Christ, you will live like that.

Focusing on the Facts

1. What can be said about habitual liars (see p. 37)?
2. Why do people lie (see p. 38)?
3. How does a person's life change with regard to truth when he becomes a Christian (see p. 38)?
4. Cite different ways people lie (see p. 38).
5. Why is it important for Christians to tell the truth (see p. 39)?
6. What three Greek words are translated "anger"? Define each (see p. 40).
7. What kind of anger should never characterize a Christian? Why (see p. 40)?
8. What kind of anger is tolerable for Christians? Explain (see pp. 40-41).
9. Cite some examples of people who exemplified righteous anger (see p. 41).
10. The wrong kind of anger is the first step toward _____ (Matt. 5:21-22; see p. 41).
11. What should believers do when their anger turns to sin (Eph. 4:26; see p. 42)?
12. What different forms of stealing does the Bible discuss (see p. 43)?
13. What does Scripture teach about work (see pp. 43-44)?
14. Why ought Christians work hard (see p. 44)?

15. Explain what "corrupt communication" is (Eph. 4:29; see p. 44).
16. What is the source of corrupt communication (see p. 45)?
17. What characterizes good speech? Explain each one (Eph. 4:29; see pp. 45-46).
18. What makes the Holy Spirit grieve? What should motivate us not to grieve Him (see p. 46)?
19. Cite and define the natural vices Paul refers to in Ephesians 4:31 (see p. 47).
20. What are the supernatural graces (Eph. 4:32; see p. 47)?

Pondering the Principles

1. Review the various kinds of lies (see p. 38). Note that some lies are subtle. Make a list of those kinds of lies, plus any others you can think of. Next to each, indicate if you have lied in that way since you became a Christian. Also indicate if you are presently engaged in one or more of those lies. If so, what do you intend to do about it? Ephesians 4:25 says we are to speak the truth with our neighbor. Therefore if you have recently betrayed a confidence, you need to go to that person and confess what you have done. Telling the truth can be painful at times, but it is the right thing to do, and God will bless your obedience to His Word.

2. Although it is comforting to know there is a biblical basis for some anger, if we're honest with ourselves we have to admit that most of our anger is the result of sin. Review the kinds of anger (pp. 40-41). Are you angry about something or at someone right now? How do you normally handle your anger? The next time you become angry in a sinful manner, follow the exhortation of Ephesians 4:26: don't carry your anger into the next day. Instead, confess it right away. If need be, go to the person you were angry with and confess your sin. Make it your goal to deal with your anger, and don't give the devil an opportunity to wreak havoc in your life.

3. According to Ephesians 4:28, why are we to work with our hands? Is that your motive as you work, or is it your goal to satisfy your needs exclusively? When you receive a raise, what do you do with the additional income? How do you use your discretionary income (that which is above what you need to meet

49

your basic needs)? Make a careful examination of your answers to those questions. If you are continually seeking a better home, a better car, better clothes, and better possessions, it's possible that you are not looking to advance God's kingdom. Reflect on Matthew 6:19-33, and ask God to help you see what changes in priorities you need to make.

4. Are most of your conversations edifying, necessary, and gracious? After your next conversation, reflect on what you said. What parts were edifying, necessary, and gracious? What parts were not? So that you might glorify God in all your conversations, memorize Ephesians 4:29: "Let no unwholesome word proceed from your mouth, but only such a word as is good for edification according the need of the moment, that it may give grace to those who hear" (NASB*).

* *New American Standard Bible.*

4
Walking in Love—Part 1

Outline

Introduction
A. The Concept of Imitating God
   1. The pursuit
   2. The paradox
     a) Stated
     b) Resolved
B. The Structure of Ephesians
   1. The application
   2. The blessings

Lesson
I. The Plea (vv. 1-2*a*)
  A. The Context
    1. The opposite characteristic of love
    2. The obvious characteristics of love
  B. The Commentary
    1. The measure of love
      a) The demonstration of love
        (1) In God's plan of salvation
        (2) In Christ's payment for sin
      b) The degree of love
      c) The depth of love
        (1) The indicators
        (2) The illustration
    2. The practice of love
    3. The characteristics of love
      a) Toward God
        (1) It is loyal
        (2) It is faithful

Introduction

Ephesians 5:1-7 touches on the heart of the Christian life: the subject of love. Verse 2 says, "Walk in love." There is no more beautiful or direct definition of how Christians are to live. Love is so important that if it is not visible in a person's life, there is good reason to doubt his or her salvation. Verse 5 says, "No fornicator, nor unclean person, nor covetous man (who is an idolater) hath any inheritance in the kingdom of Christ and of God." Verse 6 indicates there are people who attempt to deceive God's people by selling the world's counterfeit love, which involves fornication, adultery, covetousness, and uncleanness.

However, true Christians will not be characterized by counterfeit love. Instead they will follow the pattern of 1 John 4:7-8, which says, "Beloved, let us love one another; for love is of God, and everyone that loveth is born of God, and knoweth God. He that loveth not knoweth not God; for God is love." If a person is not characterized by love, he doesn't know God.

A. The Concept of Imitating God

Ephesians 5:1 says, "Be ye, therefore, followers of God, as dear children." The Greek word translated "followers" is *mimētai*, from which we get the English word *mimic*. We are

52

to be mimics of God. A mimic does not pick up general patterns of another person; he copies specific characteristics.

1. The pursuit

    The Christian life could be summed up in this one statement: be mimics, or imitators, of God.

    a) Matthew 5:48—Jesus said, "Be ye, therefore, perfect, even as your Father, who is in heaven, is perfect."

    b) 1 Peter 1:15-16—Peter said, "As he who hath called you is holy, so be ye holy in all manner of life, because it is written, Be ye holy; for I am holy."

    c) 1 Corinthians 11:1—Paul said, "Be ye followers of me, even as I also am of Christ."

    d) 2 Corinthians 3:18—Paul also said, "We all, with unveiled face beholding as in a mirror the glory of the Lord, are changed into the same image from glory to glory, even as by the Spirit of the Lord."

    e) 1 John 3:2—The ultimate hope of the Christian life is knowing that "when he [Christ] shall appear, we shall be like him; for we shall see him as he is."

    The more you know God the more you'll understand what He wants you to be, so the primary pursuit of any believer is to know God (Phil. 3:10). That can be achieved only when we study God's character as it is revealed in Scripture.

    Please note that imitating God is not just a New Testament principle. As far back as Leviticus 11:45 God said, "Be holy, for I am holy."

2. The paradox

    a) Stated

        Imitating God may be easy to discuss, but it is difficult to do. You cannot do it in your own strength. But Jesus gave us the starting point for imitating God in

53

the Sermon on the Mount. We need to mourn over our sin with a broken and contrite spirit. When we are overwhelmed by our sinfulness, we will hunger and thirst for righteousness. So there is a paradox: we are to be like God, yet we must know we cannot be like Him on our own.

b) Resolved

Once we are aware of the paradox, we know there must be some other power to make imitating God a possibility. The apostle Paul prayed that God would strengthen us "with might by his Spirit in the inner man" (Eph. 3:16). The Holy Spirit provides the strength "that ye might be filled with all the fullness of God" (v. 19). We can be like God (in terms of His character), but we can't do it on our own—that is the Spirit's work.

B. The Structure of Ephesians

1. The application

The first three chapters of Ephesians deal with doctrine and the last three with the practical ramifications of that doctrine. The practical section begins as Paul says, "I therefore, the prisoner of the Lord, beseech you that ye walk worthy of the vocation to which ye are called" (Eph. 4:1). The last three chapters emphasize the Christian walk, which is to be a worthy walk.

What does the worthy walk involve? Walking in humility (4:1-3), unity (4:4-16), newness (4:17-32), love (5:1-7), light (5:8-14), wisdom (5:15-17), and the Spirit (5:18–6:9); it also involves spiritual warfare (6:10-24).

At the heart of the discussion comes the phrase "Be ye . . . followers of God" (5:1). That ties all the elements together. Since God humbled Himself in Christ, we are to be humble. Since the Trinity is three yet one, we must be one with other believers. Since God is different—set apart from this evil world—we should be different. Since God is love, we are to be love. Since God is light, we can be light. Since God is wise, we should be wise.

Since God is spiritual, we should be directed by spiritual principles. And since God is the victor over Satan, we are to have victory over him as well.

2. The blessings

The first three chapters of Ephesians delineate the blessings we have in Christ. We have a new standing before God (1:4), a new life (2:4-6), a new righteousness (1:7), a new Father (1:5), a new inheritance (1:11, 14, 18), a new citizenship (2:6, 19), a new Master (1:22-23), a new freedom (3:12), a new victory (2:1-7), a new security (1:13), a new peace (2:14-18), a new unity (2:14-18), a new fellowship (2:19), a new joy (1:3), a new Spirit (2:22), a new power (3:20), a new ability (3:16-19), a new calling (2:10), a new purpose (3:10-12), and a new love (3:17).

The concept of love is woven throughout those chapters. God predestined us to love (1:4-5). He loved us with His great love (2:4). And we can "know the love of Christ, which passeth knowledge" (3:19). Our position in Christ is predicated on God's love. First Corinthians 13:13 says, "Now abideth faith, hope, love, these three; but the greatest of these is love." Since God is love (1 John 4:16), and since we are to imitate Him, Paul commands us to "walk in love."

Lesson

I. THE PLEA (vv. 1-2*a*)

"Be ye, therefore, followers of God, as dear children; and walk in love."

A. The Context

The word "therefore" takes us backward in the epistle.

1. The opposite characteristic of love

Ephesians 4:31 says, "Let all bitterness, and wrath, and anger, and clamor, and evil speaking, be put away from you, with all malice." Those are the opposite of love. When we are bitter toward someone, violent, or smoldering internally about someone or something, or slandering someone publicly or behind his back, that's the opposite of walking in love.

2. The obvious characteristics of love

Verse 32 says, "Be ye kind one to another, tenderhearted, forgiving one another." Those are characteristics of love. Of those three, the greatest evidence of love is forgiveness. A lack of forgiveness causes bitterness, wrath, anger, slander, and all forms of malice. And a lack of forgiveness stems from a lack of love.

Paul doesn't refer to love in verse 32, but he does mention kindness, tenderheartedness, and forgiveness. To be certain we remember where those characteristics come from, he tells us to imitate God by walking in love. The key to walking in love is forgiveness.

B. The Commentary

1. The measure of love

I believe the greatest measuring rod of love in the life of a Christian is forgiveness.

a) The demonstration of love

(1) In God's plan of salvation

God showed His love to us in terms of forgiveness. The Bible could have taught us that God so loved the world that He made pretty flowers or trees or mountains, or beautiful ladies, or handsome men, or delicious food. Rather it teaches that "God so loved the world that he gave his only begotten Son, that whosoever believeth in him should not perish, but have everlasting life" (John 3:16). He gave His Son to forgive mankind. That certainly shows us God's love more than flowers, trees, or mountains.

56

The best measurement of a person's love is his ability to forgive. That's because the best measurement of God's love is His ability to forgive. Ephesians 2:5 says, "Even when we were dead in sins, [God] hath made us alive together with Christ." Why? Because "God . . . is rich in mercy, for his great love with which he loved us" (v. 4).

Measure your love. Ask yourself, *Do I love?* If you don't, you are not one of God's own because the children of God love others (1 John 4:7-8). How can you know whether you are characterized by love? Ask yourself, *Am I bitter toward someone because of something he did to me? Do I often get angry with people, either externally or internally? Do I speak maliciously behind people's backs? Do I verbally assault people?* Those are characteristics of our old lifestyle—characteristics we must get rid of.

(2) In Christ's payment for sin

We are to forgive "as God, for Christ's sake, hath forgiven you" (Eph. 4:32). No matter what others do to you—whether they hurt, slander, wound, or offend you—Christ has already paid the penalty for their sin. The next time you want to make someone suffer for what he has done to you, remember that Christ already suffered for that sin. Don't add to the suffering and consequence that has resulted from that sin—it's already been dealt with.

You and I offend God more than we realize, but He doesn't punish those offenses by giving us what we deserve—eternal punishment. Instead His Son already bore the punishment for those sins. For Christ's sake He forgives us. And for Christ's sake we are to forgive each other. So the measure of your love is the extent of your ability to forgive.

b) The degree of love

At times it may seem that you just cannot go on for-giving someone who does the same thing over and over again. But God keeps on forgiving us.

(1) 1 John 2:12—"Little children . . . your sins are forgiven you for his name's sake."

(2) Colossians 2:13—God has "forgiven you all tres-passes."

(3) Ephesians 1:7—"In [Christ] we have redemption through his blood, the forgiveness of sins."

(4) 1 John 1:9—"If we confess our sins, he is faithful and just to forgive us our sins, and to cleanse us from all unrighteousness."

God keeps forgiving us even though we continue to sin, and He expects us to do the same to others. If our holy, righteous God can forgive someone's sin and put it on His dear Son, who are we to demand blood out of that person? But that's just what we're doing when we refuse to forgive him or her.

c) The depth of love

Two important factors indicate the depth of your love.

(1) The indicators

(*a*) How much you forgive

Proverbs 10:12 says, "Love covereth all sins." First Peter 4:8 says, "Above all things have fervent love among yourselves; for love shall cover the multitude of sins." The Greek word translated "fervent" (*ektenēs*) refers to a mus-cle stretched to its limits. We are to love to the limit, which involves covering a "multitude of sins." Sin must be dealt with but must also be forgiven. That's what "cover" implies. We're to put a blanket over past sin that has been dealt with.

Examine yourself. Do you hold a grudge against someone in your house? If you do, remember that Jesus already paid the penalty for whatever that person did wrong. Your inability to forgive belies your love. And if a lack of forgiveness is characteristic of your life, you may not be a Christian.

(b) How much you know you've been forgiven

Inevitably those who have the greatest sense of forgiveness are quickest to forgive others. Smug self-righteous people usually have the most trouble forgiving someone for a sordid past. But the former alcoholic, prostitute, or criminal often looks at someone else's sin and says, "You ought to forgive that person. Look what the Lord did for me!" Some who have gone to church all their lives look down on those with evil pasts. Yet the sin of religious piety is just as bad as, if not worse than, prostitution. The people who know they've been forgiven much are able to forgive much.

(2) The illustration

Luke 7:36-48 contrasts a Pharisee with a sinful woman.

(a) The love of the sinner

Verses 36-38 begin the narrative: "One of the Pharisees desired . . . that [Jesus] would eat with him. And he went into the Pharisee's house, and sat down to eat. And, behold, a woman in the city, who was a sinner [possibly a prostitute], when she knew that Jesus was eating in the Pharisee's house, brought an alabaster box of [costly] ointment, and stood at his feet behind him, weeping [mourning over her sin]; and began to wash his feet with tears, and did wipe them with the hair of her head, and kissed his feet, and anointed them with the ointment."

(b) The sin of the Pharisee

If she had done the same thing to the Pharisee, he probably would have slapped her across the mouth and had one of his servants throw her into the street. We see his attitude in verse 39: "When the Pharisee who had bidden him saw it, he spoke within himself, saying, This man, if he were a prophet, would have known who and what manner of woman this is that toucheth him; for she is a sinner."

(c) The parable of Christ

Jesus responded to the Pharisee's thoughts: "Simon, I have somewhat to say unto thee. And he saith, Master, say on. There was a certain creditor who had two debtors: the one owed five hundred denarii, and the other fifty. And when they had nothing to pay, he frankly forgave them both. Tell me, therefore, which of them will love him most? Simon answered, and said, I suppose that he to whom he forgave most. And he said unto him, Thou hast rightly judged. And he turned to the woman, and said unto Simon, Seest thou this woman? I entered into thine house; thou gavest me no water for my feet. But she hath washed my feet with tears, and wiped them with the hair of her head. Thou gavest me no kiss. But this woman, since the time I came in, hath not ceased to kiss my feet. My head with oil thou didst not anoint. But this woman hath anointed my feet with ointment. Wherefore, I say unto thee, Her sins, which are many, are forgiven; for she loved much. But to whom little is forgiven, the same loveth little" (vv. 40-47).

The woman responded to Jesus the way she did because she loved Him very much. She loved Him so deeply because she was keenly aware of her sin and sought great forgiveness. So Jesus turned to her and said, "Thy sins are forgiven" (v. 48). One's ability to love depends on how deeply one senses the love of God, and one's ability to forgive depends on how much one knows he has been forgiven. Apparently the smug Pharisee thought he was so righteous that he didn't need forgiveness. He wasn't interested in washing Jesus' feet or in serving Him; he was interested only in a theological discussion. He couldn't forgive the woman because he had such a dull sense of sin and his need for forgiveness. If the Pharisee and the woman compared their sin, the Pharisee's would have been greater because it is an unparalleled sin to say, "I don't need God."

A person who loves little doesn't sense God's love. The person who loves much does.

2. The practice of love

God loved us and forgave us, and He expects us to do the same for each other. In that sense we are to be like God, and it is the Spirit who helps us accomplish that. Nevertheless it is easy for us to respond like Zophar: "Canst thou by searching find out God?" (Job 11:7). How can we be like God? It seems impossible. If we saw Him as a benign Santa Claus, perhaps we could be like Him. But if we understand God as the Bible defines Him, we must say with Peter, "Depart from me; for I am a sinful man, O Lord" (Luke 5:8). Or we might follow the example of John who, seeing a vision of the exalted Christ, "fell at his feet as dead" (Rev. 1:17).

We are to be as merciful (Luke 6:36), holy (1 Pet. 1:15), perfect (Matt. 5:48), and loving (1 John 4:11) as God. How is that possible?

Second Peter 1:4 says that when we were regenerated we became "partakers of the divine nature." We can be like God because He lives in us. It is also possible by sanctification: as the Spirit of God works in our lives, He conforms us to His image (Eph. 3:17-19).

In Ephesians 5:1 Paul is saying that if you are a child of God, you should act like one. If you name Jesus as Lord, walk as He walked. First John 2:6 says, "He that saith he abideth in him ought himself also so to walk, even as he walked." We find a good summary of the matter in 1 Corinthians 16:14: "Let all your things be done with love." Love should characterize everything we do in life.

3. The characteristics of love

Love has always been God's standard. In fact, although they appear to be crushing legalism on the surface, the Ten Commandments are in reality ten commands to love. The first four commands delineate the characteristics of love toward God; the latter six describe love toward others.

a) Toward God

(1) It is loyal

Exodus 20:3 says, "Thou shalt have no other gods before me." Love isn't fickle; it's loyal. God wants us to love Him enough not to leave Him for someone or something else. If we love Him, we won't bow down to other gods or turn our backs on the one true God.

(2) It is faithful

Exodus 20:4-6 says, "Thou shalt not make unto thee any carved image, or any likeness of anything that is in heaven above, or that is in the earth beneath, or that is in the water under the earth; thou shalt not bow down thyself to them, nor serve them; for I, the Lord thy God, am a jealous God, visiting the iniquity of the fathers upon the children unto the third and fourth generation of them that hate me; and showing mercy unto thousands of them that love me, and keep my commandments." If you love God, you'll never leave Him; you will remain faithful.

(3) It is reverent

In verse 7 God says, "Thou shalt not take the name of the Lord thy God in vain; for the Lord will not hold him guiltless that taketh his name in vain." If you love God you won't besmirch His reputation.

(4) It is intimate

Exodus 20:8-11 says, "Remember the sabbath day, to keep it holy. Six days shalt thou labor and do all thy work; but the seventh day is the sabbath of the Lord thy God; in it thou shalt not do any work, thou, nor thy son, nor thy daughter, thy manservant, nor thy maidservant, nor thy cattle, nor thy stranger that is within thy gates; for in six days the Lord made heaven and earth, the sea, and all that in them is, and rested the seventh day; wherefore, the Lord blessed the sabbath day, and hallowed it." God's love draws us aside for intimacy with Him. It's as if God is saying, "If you love Me, you won't live your life apart from Me; instead you'll draw near to Me. You'll be willing to drop all your activities one day a week and spend it with Me."

Our love toward God is to be loyal, faithful, reverent, and intimate. Jesus summed that up in these words: "Thou shalt love the Lord thy God with all thy heart, and with all thy soul, and with all thy mind, and with all thy strength" (Mark 12:30).

b) Toward others

(1) It is respectful

Exodus 20:12 says, "Honor thy father and thy mother, that thy days may be long upon the land which the Lord thy God giveth thee." Love is not lawless or rebellious; it is respectful—it honors people. An individual characterized by love attempts to say the best about everyone. He seeks to help and honor others.

(2) It is harmless

Verse 13 says, "Thou shalt not kill." Someone who truly loves does not seek to hurt others.

(3) It is pure

Verse 14 says, "Thou shalt not commit adultery." Adultery defiles, but love purifies.

(4) It is unselfish

Verse 15 says, "Thou shalt not steal." People who love do not steal; they give.

(5) It is truthful

Verse 16 says, "Thou shalt not bear false witness against thy neighbor." When you tell a lie about someone, you are trying to hurt him. But if you love him, you tell the truth.

(6) It is content

Exodus 20:17 says, "Thou shalt not covet thy neighbor's house; thou shalt not covet thy neighbor's wife, nor his manservant, nor his maidservant, nor his ox, nor his ass, nor anything that is thy neighbor's." A person who loves others is content with his own possessions and is happy for whatever blessings others receive.

Our love toward others is to be respectful, harmless, pure, unselfish, truthful, and content. Jesus summed that up when He said, "Thou shalt love thy neighbor as thyself" (Mark 12:31). The Ten Commandments teach us to be like God. We are to love as He loves.

II. THE PATTERN (v. 2*b*)

"As Christ also hath loved us, and hath given himself for us an offering and a sacrifice to God for a sweet-smelling savor."

A. The Characteristics of Christ's Love

Christ Himself is our pattern. If we are to love as He loves us, then we need to know the characteristics of His love.

1. It is forgiving

When Jesus died on the cross He said of those who crucified Him, "Father, forgive them" (Luke 23:34).

2. It is unconditional

The Bible doesn't refer to Christian love as an emotion but as an act of self-sacrifice. A person who truly loves someone else doesn't try to get anything out of that person. Do you realize that God loves people who are on their way to hell as much as He loves those on their way to heaven? He loves those who curse Him as much as those who praise Him. Why? Because God's love is never conditioned upon a response—it is unconditional.

The world often defines love in terms of what it can get. But God loves even if He never gets anything in return. If that kind of love characterized our marriages, the divorce rate wouldn't be what it is today. If those who claim they don't love their spouses anymore would commit themselves to loving them unconditionally, they just might find they can recapture or rebuild their love. Our Lord Jesus Christ doesn't love us for what He can get out of us; He loves us in spite of the hurt we cause Him. Unconditional love is humble, obedient, and self-sacrificing.

3. It is self-sacrificing

Ephesians 5:2 says that Christ "hath given himself for us an offering and a sacrifice to God for a sweet-smelling savor." Christ's sacrificial offering of Himself was a fragrant aroma to God. Paul described a gift he received as "an odor of a sweet smell, a sacrifice acceptable, well-pleasing to God" (Phil. 4:18). That Christ's offering of Himself was sweet smelling meant that God was well pleased with it.

Leviticus 1-3 describes three types of offerings Israel was to make: the burnt offering, the meal offering, and the peace offering. If we view Christ's work in light of those offerings, we could say that the burnt offering refers to Christ's total devotion to God—He gave His life. The meal offering refers to His perfection. And the peace offering speaks of His making peace between God and man. Those three offerings were well pleasing to God.

Do you want to please God? Do you want your life to rise before God as a sweet-smelling aroma? Then live a life of forgiving, unconditional, and self-sacrificing love.

Focusing on the Facts

1. What does it mean to be "followers" of God (Eph. 5:1; see pp. 52-53)?
2. What ought to be the primary pursuit of believers (Phil. 3:10; see p. 53)?
3. What must we first realize before we can imitate God (see pp. 53-54)?
4. How can we be like God (Eph. 3:16, 19; see p. 54)?
5. What does the worthy walk referred to in Ephesians 4:1 involve (see p. 54)?
6. What has God given to us in Christ (see p. 55)?
7. In what way is the concept of love woven throughout the first three chapters of Ephesians (see p. 55)?
8. What is the great measuring rod of love in the life of a Christian (see p. 56)?
9. How can we measure God's love (Eph. 2:4-5; see p. 57)?
10. What ought to be our motive for forgiving others (Eph. 4:32; see p. 57)?
11. What are two indicators of the depth of a person's love (see pp. 58-59)?
12. What does love do according to 1 Peter 4:8 (see p. 58)?

13. What is often true about people who have a great sense of how much they have been forgiven (see p. 59)?
14. According to Luke 7:39, what was the attitude of the Pharisee toward the woman who washed Jesus' feet (see p. 60)?
15. How did Jesus respond to his attitude (Luke 7:40-47; see pp. 60-61)?
16. Why did the woman treat Jesus in the way she did? Why did the Pharisee treat Jesus in the way he did (see p. 61)?
17. How is it possible to be as merciful, holy, perfect, and loving as God (see pp. 61-62)?
18. What aspects of love do each of the Ten Commandments describe (see pp. 62-64)?
19. What are three characteristics of Christ's love? Explain each (see pp. 65-66).

Pondering the Principles

1. Before we can imitate God, we must know what He is like. Like Paul, that is to be our primary desire (Phil. 3:10). Jesus said, "This is life eternal, that they might know thee, the only true God, and Jesus Christ, whom thou hast sent" (John 17:3). The best way for us to know God better is to do the same thing we would do if we wanted to get to know anyone—spend time with Him. The best way to do that is to spend time in His Word. By daily exposure to what God has taught us about Himself, we will learn what He is like. Make sure you regularly read and study the Bible. Make note of any passages that give you insight into God's character.

2. Review the section on the depth of love (pp. 58-61). How much do you actually forgive others? If you haven't forgiven certain people, what reason do you offer for not having done so? After studying this chapter, is there any justifiable reason for not forgiving them? Be honest with yourself in your analysis. Ask God to reveal your sin to you, and then confess it to Him. Now look back over your life, both before you came to Christ and after. For what has God forgiven you? Make a list if that will help you remember. Once you've completed your list, write *Forgiven* across the list. Take the time to thank God for that all He has forgiven you. And thank Him for His plan of salvation and the sacrifice of His Son on your behalf.

5
Walking in Love—Part 2

Outline

Review
I. The Plea (vv. 1-2*a*)
II. The Pattern (v. 2*b*)
   A. The Characteristics of Christ's Love

Lesson
   B. An Example of Christ's Love
      1. The setting
      2. The service
      3. The sermon
III. The Perversion (vv. 3-4)
   A. The World's Search for Love
      1. The forgiving master
      2. The unforgiving servant
   B. The World's Kind of Love
      1. Unholy deeds
        a) "Fornication"
          (1) Its antonym
          (2) Its usage
        b) "Uncleanness"
        c) "Covetousness"
      2. Unholy speech
        a) "Filthiness"
        b) "Foolish talking"
        c) "Jesting"
IV. The Punishment (vv. 5-6)
   A. The Recipients of Punishment (v. 5)
   B. The Reason for Punishment (v. 6)

Conclusion

Review

Ephesians 4-6 is Paul's discussion of the worthy walk. An important aspect of it is to walk in love (5:2). Walking in love has four elements.

I. THE PLEA (vv. 1-2*a*; see pp. 55-64)

"Be ye, therefore, followers of God, as dear children; and walk in love."

Children Make the Best Mimics

Notice that verse 1 says we are to be "followers of God, as dear children." The basis for imitating God is that we are His children. First Peter 1:23 says we have been "born again, not of corruptible seed, but of incorruptible, by the word of God, which liveth and abideth forever." Since God made us His children (Eph. 1:5), we ought to manifest His characteristics. Galatians 3:26 says, "Ye are all the sons of God by faith in Christ Jesus." When you put your faith in Christ and received Him as Savior, you became a child of God; you were born again (John 3:3). As a result it would be abnormal for you not to imitate God. In the physical realm, it is normal for a child to be like his parents. The same is true in the spiritual realm. Galatians 4:4-7 says, "When the fullness of time was come, God sent forth his Son, made of a woman, made under the law, to redeem them that were under the law, that we might receive the adoption of sons. And because ye are sons, God hath sent forth the Spirit of his Son into your hearts, crying, Abba, Father. Wherefore, thou art no more a servant, but a son; and if a son, then an heir of God through Christ." When you were saved you became a child of God. His Spirit is now in you, and your life should manifest the life of God.

II. THE PATTERN (v. 2*b*)

"As Christ also hath loved us, and hath given himself for us an offering and a sacrifice to God for a sweet-smelling savor."

A. The Characteristics of Christ's Love (see pp. 65-66)

When I was a child starting out in school, I learned how to draw by tracing bold images on tracing paper. Similarly, Christ is our pattern. The apostle Paul said to Timothy, "Be thou an example of the believers" (1 Tim. 4:12). Timothy was to be someone other believers could pattern their lives after. If we are to love as God loves, we must be willing to forgive others and love them unconditionally and sacrificially. Jesus met each of those conditions when He died on the cross.

Lesson

B. An Example of Christ's Love

John 13 contains perhaps the most beautiful picture of Christ's love apart from His death on the cross. Here we can see His unconditional, forgiving, and self-sacrificing love in action.

1. The setting

The setting is the Upper Room on the night before Jesus' crucifixion. The disciples were arguing about who would be the greatest in the kingdom. Jesus was about to be crucified, yet they were indifferent to what He was about to endure. They didn't realize the sinless Son of God was about to bear in His body the sins of every person who ever lived. They didn't even care because they were selfish, sinful, and unresponsive to His needs. If they had loved Him as they claimed, they would have been comforting and encouraging.

In Jesus' time it was customary for a servant to wash everyone's feet before the meal because the people ate on the floor and one diner's head was always at another's feet. Since no servant was present, it would have been appropriate for one of the disciples to take on the role of a servant and wash the others' feet. But they were too busy arguing about who would be the greatest in the kingdom. So supper began without anyone's feet being washed.

2. The service

Notice what happens in John 13:4-5: "[Jesus] riseth from supper, and laid aside his garments, and took a towel, and girded himself. After that he poureth water into a basin, and began to wash the disciples' feet, and to wipe them with the towel with which he was girded." Now that is love in action! The disciples were full of pride and self-centered. They resented each other, knowing that each was seeking a higher position for himself. In the midst of that sinful arena, Jesus washed their feet in a kind, tender, and sympathetic act. He didn't even ask for a response from them. What an example of forgiving, unconditional, self-sacrificing love!

3. The sermon

Jesus summed up His example by saying, "Ye call me Master and Lord; and ye say well; for so I am. If I, then, your Lord and Master, have washed your feet, ye also ought to wash one another's feet. For I have given you an example, that ye should do as I have done to you. Verily, verily, I say unto you, The servant is not greater than his lord; neither he that is sent greater than he that sent him. If ye know these things, happy are ye if ye do them" (vv. 13-17).

Later that evening He said to them, "A new commandment I give unto you, that ye love one another; as I have loved you, that ye also love one another. By this shall all men know that ye are my disciples, if ye have love one to another" (vv. 34-35). Jesus commanded them to love as He had loved them. And He had just demonstrated forgiving, unconditional, and self-sacrificing love. That's the kind of love we're to have for each other.

III. THE PERVERSION (vv. 3-4)

Whatever God establishes, Satan will counterfeit. In Ephesians 5:3-6 we see how Satan attempts to pervert God's love.

A. The World's Search for Love

The people of the world want love very much. In fact, the only thing they want more than love is money. Loving, being loved, and making love are viewed as the ultimate high. Love is seen as the way to experience emotional extremes: you'll never be as happy nor as sad as when you're in love.

Today's music feeds that quest for love. Throughout much of it is the same underlying message: either the fantasy of a love sought or the despair of a love lost. People continue to chase that elusive dream. They base their concept of love on what it does for them. Songs, plays, films, books, and TV programs continually perpetuate the fantasy—the dream of a perfect love perfectly fulfilled.

People search for love as Ponce de Leon searched for the fountain of youth. As they look, they give themselves to other people only for what they can get. When they're no longer satisfied, they move on and find others who can satisfy them. The world's love is unforgiving, conditional, and self-centered—the very opposite of God's love. People in the world search for love, but it's not true love; it is Satan's perversion.

In Matthew 18 the Lord illustrates the world's love with a parable. Peter came to Christ and asked Him this question: "Lord, how often shall my brother sin against me, and I forgive him? Till seven times? Jesus saith unto him, I say not unto thee, Until seven times; but, Until seventy times seven" (vv. 21-22).

1. The forgiving master

Our Lord then gave the following parable: "Therefore is the kingdom of heaven likened unto a certain king, who would take account of his servants. And when he had begun to reckon, one was brought unto him, who owed him ten thousand talents. But forasmuch as he had nothing with which to pay, his lord commanded him to be sold, and his wife, and children, and all that he had, and payment to be made. The servant, therefore, fell down, and worshiped him, saying, Lord, have patience

73

with me, and I will pay thee all. Then the lord of that servant was moved with compassion, and loosed him, and forgave him the debt" (vv. 23-27). The gracious master represents God, and the indebted servant represents sinful man. The sinner comes to God on the basis of his works, claiming he can pay God back for all his sin. In spite of such a foolish claim, God is generous enough to forgive.

2. The unforgiving servant

Verse 28 continues the parable: "But the same servant went out, and found one of his fellow servants, who owed him an hundred denarii [about three months' wages]; and he laid hands on him and took him by the throat, saying, Pay me what thou owest. And his fellow servant fell down at his feet, and besought him, saying, Have patience with me, and I will pay thee all. And he would not, but went and cast him into prison, till he should pay the debt. So when his fellow servants saw what was done, they were very sorry, and came and told unto their lord all that was done. Then his lord, after he had called him, said unto him, O thou wicked servant, I forgave thee all that debt, because thou besoughtest me! Shouldest not thou also have had compassion on thy fellow servant, even as I had pity on thee? And his lord was angry, and delivered him to the inquisitors, till he should pay all that was due unto him. So likewise shall my heavenly Father do also unto you, if ye, from your hearts, forgive not every one his brother his trespasses" (vv. 28-35).

God has provided forgiveness for the sins of all the ungodly, yet some never appropriate His forgiveness. The evidence against the wicked servant is this: he was never a true believer because he never loved. Instead he responded in the typical fashion of ungodly people—with no forgiveness. The world is not forgiving; it bases its responses on whether certain conditions are met.

B. The World's Type of Love

Ephesians 5:3-4 says, "But fornication, and all uncleanness, or covetousness, let it not be once named among you, as becometh saints; neither filthiness, nor foolish talking, nor jesting, which are not fitting; but, rather, giving of thanks." If God's love and the love of His children is forgiving, unconditional, and self-sacrificing, you can be sure Satan will pervert that. Therefore the love of the world tends to be unforgiving, conditional, and self-centered. Worldly love focuses on desire, self-pleasure, and lust. It is shallow, selfish, sensual, and sexual.

Satan has sold that definition of love to the world, and, incredible as it seems, many Christians have fallen into the trap of believing it. Divorce and infidelity are rampant in the church today because of an unwillingness to walk in love. In Ephesians 5:1-6 Paul exhorts us to walk in God's love and then warns us about the world's love.

1. Unholy deeds

a) "Fornication"

The Greek word translated "fornication" (*porneia*) appears at least thirty-five times in its noun form in the New Testament. The verb form appears even more than that. So we can conclude that *porneia*, which refers to sexual sin of any kind, is a big problem.

(1) Its antonym

The Greek word *enkrateia*, which means "discipline" or "self-control," was considered a chief virtue in ancient Greek culture. The term, used ten times in the New Testament to refer to self-control or temperance, primarily refers to sexual self-control in secular Greek literature. It was used that way in the New Testament as well.

(a) Acts 24:25—When Paul was brought before Felix, the governor of Judea, and Drusilla, the governor's wife, he "reasoned of righteousness, self-control, and judgment to come." It was common knowledge that Felix had persuaded Drusilla to leave her first husband and become his third wife. Apparently Paul confronted Felix, who was a living illustration of one who violated God's righteousness by failing to have sexual self-control.

(b) 1 Corinthians 7:9—In reference to the unmarried and widowed Paul said, "If they cannot have self-control, let them marry; for it is better to marry than to burn." If someone has a problem with sexual self-control and he has a strong desire to get married, he or she ought to get married and not claim to have the gift of singleness.

Whereas *enkrateia* refers to sexual self-control, *porneia*, its antonym, refers to a lack of sexual self-control.

(2) Its usage

Porneia refers to sexual behavior that goes beyond the limits God sets. The term encompasses any kind of sexual sin and can refer to adultery, premarital sex, homosexuality, bestiality, pedophilia (sex with children), prostitution, and anything else that exhibits a lack of sexual self-control. The Greek word *graphē*, which means "to write," combined with *porneia*, gives us the English word *pornography*.

There's no place for any of those sins in the life of a Christian. Paul said, "Let [them] not be once named among you, as becometh saints" (Eph. 5:3). Paul said to the Corinthian church, "It is reported commonly that there is fornication among you" (1 Cor. 5:1). Instead of being broken about it, they were "puffed up, and [had] not rather mourned" (v. 2). Then he said, "Your glorying is not good. . . . I have written unto you not to keep company, if any man that is called a brother be a fornicator, or covetous, or an idolater, or a railer, or a drunkard, or an extortioner; with such an one, no, not to eat" (vv. 6, 11). Fornicators are to be put out of the church because they don't walk as children of God. Instead they are spots and blemishes on the assembly (2 Pet. 2:12-14).

b) "Uncleanness"

The Greek word translated "uncleanness" (*akatharsia*) is used eleven times in the New Testament. Jesus used it once to refer to the vile, rotten stench that occurs when a body decays (Matt. 23:27). The other ten times it is connected with sexual evil—the vile, rotten stench that accompanies sexual sin. It refers to immoral acts, thoughts, passions, and ideas. The world may pretend its immorality is love, but Paul accurately defined it as "uncleanness."

Sexual Immorality in the Church?

The contemporary obsession with sex has crept even into the church. I'm shocked and dismayed that some Christian authors have published what amounts to pornography. I've had some books sent to me that I've had to pitch in the trash. The world has sold its immorality so effectively that some associated with the church have bought into it and tried to sanctify it.

I've heard of at least one so-called "Christian" counselor who has advised couples to see each other naked before they decide to get married. That is ludicrous! Marriage isn't something clinical that can be dealt with in such a fashion. Some have even suggested that premarital sex would be beneficial for Christians before marriage. We need to remember what Ephesians 5:3 says: as Christians we must avoid any association with sexual sin if we are to be what God wants us to be.

c) "Covetousness"

The Greek word translated "covetousness" (*pleonexia*) could be translated "greediness." Exodus 20:17 says, "Thou shalt not covet thy neighbor's . . . wife." Men in our society covet other men's wives. They also covet women they see on TV, in movies, ads, magazines, or books. But that is sin, just one part of the world's counterfeit, fantasy love. Ironically many movie stars, who fill up the fantasies of so many, can't stay married themselves.

Pleonexia means "to defraud." It refers to the love of possessing. Some people will sacrifice everything for their lusts, including relationships with their spouses, children, or friends. They'll also destroy their home or their job—all in attempts to fulfill a fantasy. But they cannot fulfill their fantasy because it is only one of Satan's lies.

People often seek divorce because they claim to have fallen in love with someone else. But that's not a justification for divorce; it's a condemnation of those who seek it. It simply proves they have sinful hearts. People who divorce for that reason pile one sin onto another: first, in not loving their partners as God commanded and, second, in coveting what isn't theirs. Remember what happened when David coveted Bathsheba—one sin led to another (2 Sam. 11:1–12:23).

In Ephesians 5:3 Paul says, "Let it not be once named among you as becometh saints [*hagios*, "holy ones"]." How could holy ones be characterized by unholy love—selfish, conditional, and unforgiving love? We are set apart from that. Children of a holy God won't make a habit of doing unholy things.

2. Unholy speech

   a) "Filthiness"

   "Filthiness" refers to general obscenity, or that which is disgraceful. Ephesians 5:12 conveys the same idea: "It is a shame even to speak of things which are done of them in secret." We're not even to talk about the sexual evil that fornication, uncleanness, and covetousness refers to. So "filthiness" refers to disgraceful talk.

   In our day it is difficult to read a book or watch a television program or a film without being exposed to the garbage of the world. It's also difficult to hold conversations with certain people. Yet the Bible commands us never to indulge in a filthy conversation or disgraceful talk. We are called to holy conversations. We ought to communicate things from the mind and heart of God, not the filth of the world.

b) "Foolish talking"

The Greek word translated "foolish talking" (*mōrologia*) means "stupid talk." It refers to that which characterizes someone who is intellectually deficient. I call that category of speech "low obscenity." It is low-class, obscene, gutter talk. It is made up of senseless, profitless words with filthy connotations.

c) "Jesting"

The Greek word translated "jesting" (*eutrapelia*) means "able to turn easily." This kind of talk I call "high obscenity." A person who jests is able to turn what is said into something dirty. That kind of talk is characteristic of the late-night talk-show host who twists practically everything into filthy innuendo.

In contrast Ephesians 5:4 says we are to give thanks. It is the most unselfish thing we can do. Instead of seeking selfish things such as sexual fulfillment, give thanks instead. First Thessalonians 5:18 says, "In everything give thanks; for this is the will of God in Christ Jesus concerning you." When we are thankful for everything, we step outside ourselves, because thanksgiving is directed toward God. Express your love to God and to others. Let your life be characterized by thankfulness. Instead of taking from people, love them in a way that communicates thankfulness. Remember, God's love is unselfish and thankful, but the world's love is selfish and thankless.

IV. THE PUNISHMENT (vv. 5-6)

A. The Recipients of Punishment (v. 5)

"This ye know, that no fornicator, nor unclean person, nor covetous man (who is an idolater) hath any inheritance in the kingdom of Christ and of God."

If you live like those people, you are not saved! The lifestyle characteristic of unbelievers is not characteristic of believers. We are the children of God (v. 1), the beloved of Christ (v. 2), holy ones (v. 3), and citizens of the kingdom (v. 5). Therefore we must act in a manner consistent with our identity.

In verse 5 Paul says, "This ye know." The truth Paul is communicating is no mystery—we know better. Unfortunately some deceive themselves into believing that once someone makes a "decision for Christ" he is saved even if he's living as a fornicator or homosexual. But Scripture says that no fornicator is saved. That's not to say that no true believer will fall into the sin of fornication, but it certainly won't be a continual pattern of his life.

From the time of conversion there must be a change because repentance is essential to salvation. Titus 2:11-12 says, "The grace of God that bringeth salvation hath appeared to all men, teaching us that, denying ungodliness and worldly lusts, we should live soberly, righteously, and godly, in this present age." When we were saved we learned that we couldn't continue to live in lust and ungodliness.

When a Christian is drawn into a sin, such as fornication or filthy talk, the Lord will forgive him (1 John 1:9). But that sin will not characterize his life.

B. The Reason for Punishment (v. 6)

"Let no man deceive you with vain words; for because of these things cometh the wrath of God upon the sons of disobedience."

You shouldn't let anyone convince you that you can practice sin and still be a Christian because God will forgive you. That kind of rhetoric is vain—it's empty, meaningless, and useless. The sins referred to in verses 3-4 are damning. They don't characterize the children of God; they mark the children of disobedience.

Conclusion

Paul ended this section of Ephesians with a warning: "Be not ye, therefore, partakers [partners] with them" (v. 7). Don't join the world in its evil.

Focusing on the Facts

1. What is our basis for imitating God? Explain (see p. 70).
2. What were the disciples doing in the Upper Room the night before Jesus was crucified? What had they not done (see p. 71)?
3. What did Jesus do? What did He teach the disciples as a result (John 13:13-17, 34-35; see p. 72)?
4. Describe how people in the world today search for love (see p. 73).
5. How did Christ illustrate the world's love (see pp. 73-74)?
6. What is fornication? Contrast it with its antonym (see pp. 75-76).
7. According to 1 Corinthians 5:1-11, how did Paul want the church to deal with fornicators in the church (see p. 76)?
8. What does uncleanness refer to (see p. 77)?
9. Define and explain the sin of covetousness (see pp. 77-78).
10. What does filthiness refer to (see pp. 78-79)?
11. Compare and contrast foolish talking and jesting (see p. 79).
12. According to Ephesians 5:4, what kind of talk should characterize a believer? Explain (see p. 79).
13. What kind of people do not inherit God's kingdom? Explain (Eph. 5:5; see p. 80).

Pondering the Principles

1. Read John 13-17. How many instances can you find where Christ showed His love for the disciples? In what similar ways has Christ shown His love for you? Based on what you have learned about Christ's love for you, what changes do you need to make regarding your love for others?

2. Review the section on the world's kind of love (see pp. 74-79). In all honesty, can any of those characteristics be named in you?

The action doesn't need to be present for the sin to be active when we let it permeate our thoughts. Examine your thoughts. What do you think about? What kinds of things do you expose your mind to? Make a list of those things. Now read Philippians 4:8. Compare your list to the virtues listed there. Cross out any item that doesn't fulfill the parameters of Philippians 4:8. Now make a commitment to turn from those items you crossed off.

6
Living in the Light

Outline

Introduction
  A. The Contrast Between Light and Darkness
    1. Symbolized
      a) Light
      b) Darkness
    2. Illustrated
      a) Intellectually
      b) Morally
  B. The Character of a Christian
    1. Stated
    2. Commanded

Lesson
  I. The Contrast (v. 8)
    A. Our Past Problem
      1. We did the works of Satan
      2. We were ruled by Satan
      3. We were under the penalty of divine wrath
      4. We were sentenced to eternal darkness
    B. Our Present Privilege
  II. The Characteristics (vv. 9-10)
    A. The Fruit (v. 9)
      1. Described
        a) Goodness
        b) Righteousness
        c) Truth
      2. Demonstrated
    B. The Proof (v. 10)
  III. The Command (v. 11*a*)

IV. The Commission (vv. 11*b*-13)
   A. Expose Evil Deeds (v. 11*b*)
      1. By our life
      2. By our words
   B. Don't Speak of Shameful Things (v. 12)
   C. Bring Light to the Darkness (v. 13)
V. The Call (v. 14)

Conclusion

Introduction

The book of Ephesians presents the pattern for Christian living. The first three chapters delineate who the Christian is. The last three describe how he lives. Our behavior as Christians can be summed up in two statements: "Walk worthy" (4:1) and be "followers [imitators] of God" (5:1). If we're going to imitate God, we're going to need a pattern. Therefore verse 2 says, "Walk in love, as Christ also hath loved us." We are to be like Christ.

Walking like Christ has many facets. We've already been told we should walk in humility (4:1-3), in unity (4:4-16), in newness (4:17-32), and in love (5:1-7). In our present study we will see that we must also walk in light, for we are children of light.

A. The Contrast Between Light and Darkness

   1. Symbolized

      a) Light

         In the intellectual sense, light symbolizes truth. In the moral sense, it refers to holiness. Living in light means living in truth and in holiness.

      b) Darkness

         In contrast, darkness refers to ignorance in the intellectual sense and evil in the moral sense.

2. Illustrated

   a) Intellectually

      (1) Proverbs 6:23—"The commandment is a lamp, and the law is light." Here light refers to truth, not deeds. God's Word is intellectual truth.

      (2) Psalm 119:105—"Thy word is a lamp unto my feet and a light unto my path."

      (3) 2 Corinthians 4:3-4, 6—"If our gospel be hidden it is hidden to them that are lost, in whom the god of this age hath blinded the minds of them who believe not, lest the light of the glorious gospel of Christ, who is the image of God, should shine unto them. . . . For God, who commanded the light to shine out of darkness, hath shone in our hearts, to give the light of the knowledge of the glory of God in the face of Jesus Christ."

   b) Morally

      (1) Isaiah 5:20—"Woe unto them who call evil, good, and good, evil; who put darkness for light, and light for darkness; who put bitter for sweet, and sweet for bitter!"

      (2) Romans 13:12-13—"The night is far spent, the day is at hand; let us, therefore, cast off the works of darkness."

Intellectual darkness represents an ignorance of God and His truth, which results in moral darkness—doing evil deeds. But intellectual light represents knowledge of the truth and results in moral light—living the truth.

B. The Character of a Christian

1. Stated

A Christian walks in the light.

a) 1 John 1:5, 7—"This, then, is the message which we have heard of him, and declare unto you, that God is light, and in him is no darkness at all" (v. 5). If you are a son of God, you are a son of light. And if you are a son of light, there is no darkness in you. When you were redeemed, you were fully redeemed; there is no residual darkness. Christians don't walk in darkness. Verse 7 says, "If we walk in the light, as he is in the light, we have fellowship one with another, and the blood of Jesus Christ, his Son, cleanseth us from all sin." Look at the verse in reverse: If we have received God's forgiveness through Christ, we will have fellowship with one another and walk in the light.

b) Matthew 5:14—"Ye are the light of the world."

c) 1 Thessalonians 5:4-5—"Ye, brethren, are not in darkness. . . . Ye are all sons of light." Since God is light and He gave birth to us, we too become light.

d) Colossians 1:13—"[God] hath delivered us from the power of darkness, and hath translated us into the kingdom of his dear Son."

e) John 8:12—Jesus said, "I am the light of the world; he that followeth me shall not walk in darkness, but shall have the light of life."

There is no middle ground: when we were saved we were taken out of darkness into light. When we sin, we may do deeds of darkness, but we do them in the light; therefore they will be exposed.

2. Commanded

Ephesians 5:8 says, "Walk as children of light." Since we are children of light and since God our Father is light, we are the light of the world. As such we can't walk in darkness. Light and darkness are opposites.

We live in a dark world that's desperately in need of the light we can give it. The only way we can be effective in

86

doing that is to walk as children of light. In 2 Corinthians 6:14-15 Paul says, "What fellowship hath righteousness with unrighteousness? And what communion hath light with darkness? And what concord hath Christ with Belial?" The answer is none. Paul went on to say, "Let us cleanse ourselves from all filthiness of the flesh and spirit, perfecting holiness in the fear of God" (7:1). Since we are light, we must live like light.

Why Would Anyone Go Back in the Cave?

When a Christian sins and engages in the deeds of darkness, it's as if he has had a relapse. Imagine yourself lost in a cave. As you attempt to find your way out, you only proceed deeper and deeper into the network of tunnels. Soon you're in the belly of the earth without the slightest idea where you are. You're scared. Your heart is pounding. Your eyes are wide open, but all you can see is an oppressive blackness. You grope for hours, and the hours become a day, and then another day. Your fear mounts as all hope seems lost. Suddenly, off in the distance, there is a pinpoint of light. You move toward it, groping lest you fall into a deeper pit. Finally the light begins to widen and you find yourself at an opening in the cave! With your remaining strength you charge out into the daylight. You then know a freedom like nothing you had ever conceived was possible.

However, not long after your escape you decide there were several things you enjoyed in the cave. So you go back in. How foolish! Yet that is essentially what a Christian does when he follows after deeds of darkness.

Lesson

In Ephesians 5:8-14 Paul tells us five things we need to know if we're going to walk as children of light.

I. THE CONTRAST (v. 8)

"Ye were once darkness, but now are ye light in the Lord; walk as children of light."

A. Our Past Problem

The Greek verb translated "were" is emphatic. It emphasizes the fact that our darkness is in the past. In Ephesians 2 Paul says, "[You] were dead in trespasses and sins; in which in times past ye walked according to the course of this world, according to the prince of the power of the air, the spirit that now worketh in the sons of disobedience; among whom also we all had our manner of life in times past in the lusts of our flesh, fulfilling the desires of the flesh and of the mind, and were by nature the children of wrath, even as others. . . . Ye were without Christ, being aliens from the commonwealth of Israel, and strangers from the covenants of promise, having no hope, and without God in the world. But now in Christ Jesus ye who once were far off are made near by the blood of Christ" (vv. 1-3, 12-13). Throughout Ephesians we read of what we were without Christ and what we are in Him. We are to live what we are.

Notice that Ephesians 5:8 says, "Ye were once darkness." It doesn't say you were *in* darkness; it says you *were* darkness. You were not an innocent victim of Satan's system; you were a contributor. No worldly system of evil exists apart from the contributors to that system, be they demons or men. And no system of light exists apart from those who are the light of the world, be they Christ or His followers.

Let's look at four characteristics of our former darkness.

1. We did the works of Satan

People in the darkness do "the unfruitful works of darkness" (Eph. 5:11). They are ignorant of what is holy and don't exhibit the life of God in their hearts. Instead they do the works of Satan because he is their father (John 8:44) and "the power of darkness" (Luke 22:53).

The average non-Christian doesn't understand that he is empowered and energized by Satan. He doesn't necessarily foam at the mouth or have seven demons in him. But Satan controls him nonetheless. It's just a matter of degree. Hell will be occupied by people who were

88

energized by Satan, whether they were businessmen from Wall Street or witch doctors from Africa.

2. We were ruled by Satan

Children of Satan not only do his deeds but also are dominated by him. People will often claim they don't want to become Christians because they'll have to give up their freedom. But the only "freedom" they truly know is groping through a dark cave trying to find a way out! That's no freedom. People don't have freedom before they become Christians—they've been victimized by Satan's rule. The kingdom of darkness is ruled by the prince of darkness. And he rules the lives of all who are in the darkness.

3. We were under the penalty of divine wrath

Romans 1:18 says, "The wrath of God is revealed from heaven against all ungodliness and unrighteousness." His wrath will fall on those whose "foolish heart was darkened" (v. 21), "who exchanged the truth of God for a lie" (v. 25), and "did not like to retain God in their knowledge" (v. 28).

Jesus said, "Yet a little while is the light with you. Walk while ye have the light, lest darkness come upon you; for he that walketh in darkness knoweth not where he goeth. While ye have light, believe in the light, that ye may be the sons of light. . . . But though he had done so many miracles before them, yet they believed not on him. . . . Therefore, they could not believe, because that Isaiah said again, He hath blinded their eyes, and hardened their heart; that they should not see with their eyes, nor understand with their heart, and be converted, and I should heal them" (John 12:35-37, 39-40). When a person says he won't believe, there may come a time when God judicially confirms him in his unbelief.

4. We were sentenced to eternal darkness

Matthew 8:12 says they "shall be cast out into outer darkness; there shall be weeping and gnashing of teeth."

B. Our Present Privilege

According to Ephesians 5:8 we were once darkness, but now we are light. Paul used light and darkness—absolute opposites—to contrast what we once were with what we are. Instead of doing the works of Satan, we do the works of God: "We are his workmanship, created in Christ Jesus unto good works" (Eph. 2:10). We are no longer under the rule of Satan; we are under the lordship of Jesus Christ. We are no longer under God's wrath; we are participants in the kingdom of light. We won't go to a place of darkness; we will go to a place of light where "the Lamb is the lamp of it" (Rev. 21:23).

II. THE CHARACTERISTICS (vv. 9-10)

A. The Fruit (v. 9)

"The fruit of the [light] is in all goodness and righteousness and truth."

Many people claim they are Christians because they made a "decision" for Christ years ago, were baptized, are very religious, have gone to church for years, or have given a lot of money to the church. But the ultimate test is whether the children of light inevitably produce the fruit of light.

1. Described

a) Goodness

The fruit of goodness is a picture of how we relate to other people. Three words in the Greek language can be translated "good."

(1) *Kalos* means "free from defects" or "beautiful." It could refer to a good painting, a good jar, or a good tapestry.

(2) *Chrēstos* means "useful." It could refer to something that's good for digging a hole or good for holding things together.

(3) *Agathos* means "moral excellence." One lexicon says it is especially active on behalf of others. That is the word translated "goodness" in Ephesians 5:9. It's a goodness that touches people with a positive and morally excellent effect. In 1 Thessalonians 5:15 Paul says to do good to everyone. If you're a child of light, you ought to be good to others.

b) Righteousness

Righteousness refers to our relationship with God. We ought never to deviate from His pure path of holiness.

c) Truth

Truth can refer to integrity, honesty, reliability, or trustworthiness—anything opposed to the hypocrisy of our old life. Those are internal traits.

2. Demonstrated

If we are walking as children of light, we will exhibit the fruit of light toward others, toward God, and even in ourselves. We can determine we are in the light if we see the fruit of light in our life.

Also we can get a good idea whether people who claim to be in the light truly are. In Matthew 7 Jesus says, "Beware of false prophets, who come to you in sheep's clothing, but inwardly they are ravening wolves. Ye shall know them by their fruits. Do men gather grapes of thorns, or figs of thistles? Even so, every good tree bringeth forth good fruit" (vv. 15-17). All Christians bear fruit. Many may produce only a small yield, but there's no such thing as a Christian with no fruit. Then Jesus said, "A corrupt tree bringeth forth bad fruit. A good tree cannot bring forth bad fruit, neither can a corrupt tree bring forth good fruit. Every tree that bringeth not forth good fruit is hewn down, and cast into the fire. Wherefore, by their fruits ye shall know them" (vv. 17-20).

If you are a child of light, you will produce the fruit of light. Those who claim to be children of light but don't produce any fruit are liars or are deceived. Christians will experience a drop in fruit production when they sin, but they can't help but produce some fruit—some goodness, righteousness, and truth.

B. The Proof (v. 10)

"Proving what is acceptable unto the Lord."

We must live out the fruit of light to verify we are saved. The joy of the believer is to be a living example of God's truth—to be a living verification of what is pleasing to God.

When I was in Damascus, I discovered that the shops don't have windows. If you want to buy something, you have to take it out into the street and hold it up to the light to detect any flaws. Similarly, the only way to evaluate our lives is to expose every action, decision, and motive to the light of Christ and His Word.

When I go to the airport and put my suitcase through the X-ray machine, I never worry about what the guard might see. I don't have anything to hide. I don't carry any guns or bombs. That's the way we ought to be as Christians. We shouldn't mind having the light reveal what we are because it should only verify the truthfulness of our identity. We ought to be willing to expose our lives to light to prove that we are light.

III. THE COMMAND (v. 11a)

"Have no fellowship with the unfruitful works of darkness."

The Greek verb *koinōneō* means "fellowship." But in verse 11 Paul uses an intensified form of the verb: *sunkoinōneō*, which means "intimate fellowship." We are not to be intimately involved with "the unfruitful works of darkness"—the ignorance and immorality of the world.

However, that doesn't mean we can't talk with unsaved people. We have been commissioned to reach them with the gospel, but we must not participate in their sin. Some people have suggested that our witness would be more effective if we got involved in their sin. That's not true—it will destroy our testimony. One effective way to witness is to avoid evil deeds.

In 1 Corinthians 5:9-13 Paul tells us that we shouldn't associate with fornicators, covetors, and idolaters who claim to be Christians. But he didn't forbid us to minister to the people in the world characterized by those sins—they need us to reach out and love them. We only are commanded not to participate in their sin.

IV. THE COMMISSION (vv. 11b-13)

A. Expose Evil Deeds (v. 11b)

"But, rather, reprove them."

The Greek word translated "reprove" means "to expose." Rather than doing what people in the world do, we are to expose their evil. You could call us the spiritual CIA: our job is to expose the crimes of darkness. Our tool is the Word of God: "All Scripture is inspired by God and profitable for teaching, for *reproof*, for correction, for training in righteousness" (2 Tim. 3:16, NASB, emphasis added). Our life and our words should expose evil.

1. By our life

Sometimes just the way we live can expose the evil in people's lives. Have you ever walked up to people who know you're a Christian and who happen to be in the middle of a filthy conversation? Does it suddenly turn clean? When the non-Christians I happened to be playing golf with found out I was a pastor, their words and attitudes changed. I've known some people who lived such godly lives in the ungodly environment of their work that they were fired. They became too much of a rebuke to the system.

2. By our words

We also are commissioned by God to verbally expose the evil of the world. We must diagnose it, confront it, and then offer the solution. Sin is a cancer that must be removed. You aren't helping anyone by ignoring it. We can't politely live in the world and love people without ever acknowledging sin. That's not evangelism. People need to be convicted about their sin before they will ever see their need for a Savior.

One problem we have is that we don't see the contrast between light and darkness as dramatically as God sees it. So instead of avoiding the deeds of darkness, we may be tempted to play around with them. We should be mature enough spiritually that we search out evil and expose it, and then offer the diagnosis and cure. Unfortunately many Christians are barely able to keep themselves from darkness, let alone help others out of it. Believers need to expose evil.

B. Don't Speak of Shameful Things (v. 12)

"It is a shame even to speak of those things which are done of them in secret."

The evil deeds of the world desperately need to be reproved. The things they do are unspeakably evil. We are drowning in a sea of evil heavily promoted by the media as anything but wrong. The danger is that we can get caught up in that lie. By watching certain television programs or movies in our homes we teach our children to tolerate the very things we shouldn't even talk about. But we must not compromise; we must not even entertain evil in a conversation.

We must get beyond struggling over our sin. We need to grow up so we can reprove others and expose evil.

C. Bring Light to the Darkness (v. 13)

"All things that are reproved are made manifest by the light; for whatever doth make manifest is light."

Our commission is to expose sin in the world because we are the light. If we don't do it, it won't be exposed. No one is ever saved unless he comes to God and repents of his sin. But unbelievers won't know what sin is unless someone exposes it to them. To love people while tolerating their sin is not evangelism. True evangelism makes people face the fact of their sin. Only we can do that because we are the light of the world.

V. THE CALL (v. 14)

"Wherefore, he saith, Awake thou that sleepest, and arise from the dead, and Christ shall give thee light."

"He saith" refers to what the prophet Isaiah said in Isaiah 60:1: "Arise, shine; for thy light is come, and the glory of the Lord is risen upon thee." That verse looked forward to the Messiah, and Paul's interpretation looks back to what Christ has done.

Many Bible commentators believe that Ephesians 5:14 is a line from an Easter hymn sung by the early church. They see it as an invitation—a gospel presentation. The sinner is the one who sleeps, and the invitation is to awake and arise. The Savior is Christ, who will give light.

Like Rip Van Winkle, men and women are sleeping through an age—an age of grace. When they wake up it will be too late. So Paul encouraged them to awake and arise from the dead.

Conclusion

I remember reading of a great fire in Edinburgh where people gathered in a passageway that led to the street. They had almost reached safety when they were suddenly met by billowing smoke in the passageway. Instead of continuing through the smoke, they turned back and entered an open door. They were suddenly trapped and burned to death. If they had only seen one ray of light through the smoke, they would have lived.

Our ray of light is Jesus Christ, who said, "I am the light of the world; he that followeth me shall not walk in darkness, but shall have the light of life" (John 8:12). Horatius Bonar, in the nineteenth-century hymn "I Heard the Voice of Jesus Say," put that truth in these words:

I heard the voice of Jesus say,
"I am this dark world's Light;
Look unto Me, thy morn shall rise,
And all thy day be bright."
I looked to Jesus, and I found,
In Him my Star, my Sun;
And in that Light of life I'll walk,
Till trav'ling days are done.

Focusing on the Facts

1. What do light and darkness represent in Scripture (see p. 84)?
2. Give some examples of their use in Scripture (see p. 85).
3. What happens to believers when they are saved (Col. 1:13; see p. 86)?
4. What is the believer's relationship to darkness (Eph. 5:8; see p. 88)?
5. What four things characterize that relationship? Explain each (see pp. 88-89).
6. In contrast to our relationship to darkness, what is characteristic of our relationship to light (see p. 90)?
7. What is the fruit of the light? Describe (Eph. 5:9; see pp. 90-91).
8. What key factor did Jesus say would reveal false prophets (Matt. 7:15-20; see pp. 91-92)?
9. What proves the reality of a person's salvation (see p. 92)?
10. What command do we find in Ephesians 5:11? Explain (see p. 92).
11. With that command in mind, how can you reconcile our need to reach the unsaved with the gospel (see pp. 92-93)?
12. What are we to do to deeds of darkness? How (Eph. 5:11; see pp. 93-94)?
13. What is a problem Christians have in understanding light and darkness (see p. 94)?
14. What must unbelievers be exposed to before they can be saved? Who is responsible to do that (see pp. 94-95)?

Pondering the Principles

1. Look up the following verses: Ephesians 2:10; Colossians 1:12-13; 1 John 1:6-7; and Revelation 21:23. Those references contrast

what we have in Christ with what we were in Satan's dominion of darkness. Make note of each contrast. Thank God for each specific privilege He has granted you. How should those privileges affect your behavior as a Christian?

2. In what ways are you presently exposing evil by your life and words? It is difficult to be effective in that effort if the unbelievers you know don't know certain facts: Do unbelievers at work know you are a Christian? What about your unsaved neighbors? If you haven't accomplished this first step, begin praying for opportunities to let them know you are a Christian. Be sure you take advantage of the opportunities God gives you. Also be sure your life is consistent with God's Word; unbelievers are able to spot hypocrisy. As you do those things you'll have an opportunity to share in greater detail the ramifications of sin and the good news of the gospel.

Scripture Index

Topical Index